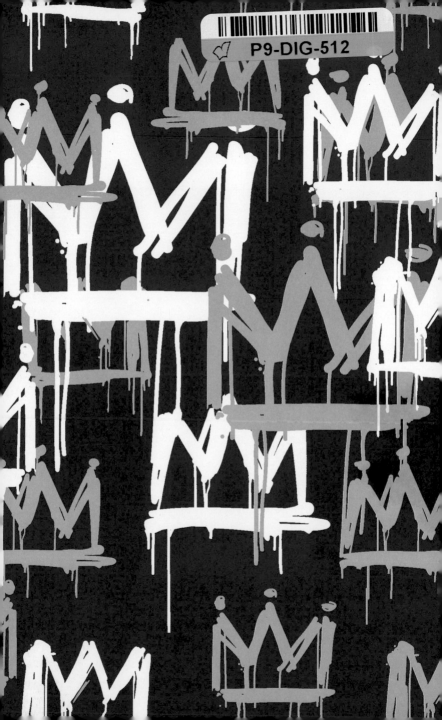

JAY-Z

Z

MADE IN AMERICA

JAY-Z

MADE IN AMERICA

MICHAEL ERIC DYSON

Illustrations by Everett Dyson

ST. MARTIN'S
PRESS
NEW YORK

First published in the United States by St. Martin's Press, an imprint of St. Martin's Publishing Group.

JAY-Z: MADE IN AMERICA. Copyright © 2019 by Michael Eric Dyson. All rights reserved. Printed in the United States of America. For information, address St. Martin's Publishing Group, 120 Broadway, New York, NY 10271.

www.stmartins.com

Designed by Steven Seighman
Endpaper art: crown © NSTdsgn/Shutterstock.com

Library of Congress Cataloging-in-Publication Data
is available upon request.

ISBN 978-1-250-23096-6 (hardcover)
ISBN 978-1-250-27088-7 (ebook)

Our books may be purchased in bulk for promotional, educational, or business use. Please contact your local bookseller or the Macmillan Corporate and Premium Sales Department at 1-800-221-7945, extension 5442, or by email at MacmillanSpecialMarkets@macmillan.com.

First Edition: November 2019

10 9 8 7 6 5 4 3 2 1

To

Robert Frederick Smith

BUSINESSMAN, INVESTOR, AND PHILANTHROPIST

*A righteous black man who embodies the best of
our people and a noble tradition of using wealth
to preserve black culture and to help the next generation
by paying off the student loan debt of nearly
400 Morehouse College graduates*

and

Michael G. Rubin

BUSINESSMAN AND PARTNER OF THE PHILADELPHIA 76ERS

*An upright man who embodies the spirit of true democracy
in the quest to reform a criminal justice system that is
fundamentally unfair to millions of black folk across the land*

It is an American cultural phenomenon, and as such, it's more than any of the definitions or connotations that I have mentioned. It's really a concept. And it's interesting to me as a writer because it's so full of contradictions. It's American, indisputably American, *and* ethnically marginal. It's black *and* free. It's intricate *and* wild. It's spontaneous *and* practiced. It's exaggerated *and* simple. It's constantly invented, always brand-new, but somehow familiar and known.

TONI MORRISON

JAY-Z portrays himself as an entrepreneur whose beginnings as a street corner crack dealer are the stuff of Horatio Alger, no less part of the mythical American Dream than corporate robber barons or big city crime bosses.

MILES WHITE

CONTENTS

FOREWORD

By Pharrell

I was honored when Michael Eric Dyson asked me to pen this foreword to his reflections on the incredible impact my dear friend and longtime collaborator JAY-Z has had on the world. Over the last quarter century, Jay has established himself as one of the most gifted artists of any genre to ever speak into a microphone. I use the idea of synesthesia to describe my approach to producing, and it's especially true when I'm working with Jay. It's the process of creating one form of sensory impression by cultivating another form of sensory impression. Art is at its best when you hear a lyric and it brings an image to mind, or when you view a painting and it makes you hear a sound. As an artist, JAY-Z really gets this simple aesthetic fact. He really does "paint pictures with poems." I am always challenged as a producer to think with my eyes, ears, and emotions when I work with Jay.

I sincerely believe that JAY-Z is a philosopher and a poet. I have likened him to the Oracle at Delphi because of his unique ability to be a prophet, seer, and mystic at the same time. These artistic attributes translate into a godlike mythology, and that vibe is captured in one of the names Jay's been given, Hova, short for JAYHOVA, a play on Jehovah. For me, it doesn't really matter who is the greatest of all MCs. That debate is arbitrary and ultimately depends on the point of view of the person arguing about the G.O.A.T. But, besides his artistic genius, there are things about Jay's career that nobody can debate. How many albums he's released, how many records he's sold, the number of hit singles he's had, the number of seats he's sold in a venue, and the number of zeroes attached to his massive material wealth. These are facts. Indeed, as Jay likes to say, they're super facts. But Jay's greatness lies beyond even the metrics of rhyme skills and material success. The numbers I've cited only matter because they represent the countless masses that greatly love and appreciate Jay's gifts. Working with him up close, I can say there is truly no one like him, and that he takes his art and craftsmanship with the utmost seriousness.

In fact, I don't mind mumble rap as much as many of its critics, mostly because I've been a witness to Jay's enigmatic and utterly astonishing writing and recording process. In studio, Jay often mumbles his way through tracks as a preparation tactic for the actual recording of his lyrics. During the mumble-rap phase of Jay's recording sessions, the lyrics to the song are indecipherable. It's a code to which only he has the key. Those of us who admire his craft can only gain access to their meaning after he blesses the microphone with the lyrical magic hidden in those well-rehearsed, yet incomprehensible, mumbles. It's a mysterious process. Even though he mumbles, Jay knows what those verses will be. It is, in effect, a lyrical exercise—a process through which he familiarizes himself with the production so that his flow will seamlessly interact with each aspect of the beat. His unmistakable flow is born in these moments, and I consider it a privilege as a producer to have been able to see quite a bit of it. JAY-Z's unparalleled writing and recording processes shed tremendous light on contemporary popular styles of an art form that he revolutionized. That is just one more example of his huge impact and his culture-defining significance.

In 2019, Jay joined me onstage for a surprise performance of several of our most popular collaborations at the "Something in the Water" music festival. I am grateful for his friendship and for every opportunity to work with him. But this performance will always have a special place in my heart and mind. "Something in the Water" is just one way that I am trying to give back to my community; it is one of the ways that I honor where I'm from, and for Jay to endorse that and support me means the world to me. But this particular performance happened in the midst of one of my home state's most tumultuous political and social periods. Still reeling from the tragedy of Charlottesville, we were faced with political crises that still remain unresolved. A month after my event, on May 31, 2019, the city of Virginia Beach experienced one of its most deadly mass shootings when an armed man entered one of our municipal buildings with the intent to murder as many innocent Virginians as possible—leaving twelve dead and many more injured. The psychological trauma is incalculable. In times like this we have to rally our communities to social justice. I have been engaged in these efforts for some time now. And I must say that Shawn "JAY-Z" Carter has been an exceptional inspiration for me in this area, just as he has been a role model for me in the music business.

For me, and I hope for you as well, *JAY-Z: Made in America* is a profound reckoning with the extraordinary musical, social, and political contributions of one of the world's greatest artists, written by one of the world's greatest public intellectuals. Dyson not only takes measure of Jay's unprecedented artistic achievements, but he uses Jay's life, lyrics, loves, and losses—and of course his spectacular triumphs—to say some important things about us as a people and a country. It is the book that hip hop and the nation need, penned by the man who can best understand what our contributions to the world mean. Even if we know all of the lyrics to all of the songs, and even if we have watched all of the videos and read all of the articles and reviews, Dyson's amazing book shows us that we still have a lot to learn about ourselves and the world we live in from the brilliant yet improbable career of a street hustler who has become a global icon.

JAY-Z

Z

MADE IN AMERICA

Each moniker that JAY-Z references serves distinct purposes related to his ability to exhibit social capital and remain fluid in the various publics in which he has influence, be it the upper echelons of the recording industry, the mainstream pop charts, Madison Avenue taste makers, or of course the "hood." . . . [T]he moniker JAY-Z is the quintessential hip-hop commodity that is at the root of the rapper's social fluidity.

MARK ANTHONY NEAL

My work is infused with [hip hop]. Actually, deeper than that, my work is grounded in it . . . I mean to say, hopefully more clearly, that if I consider my adulthood to be the time when I really began to try to think about stuff, and when I really began to think about how to think about stuff, then hip-hop is the music that was on when I embarked upon that thinking.

FRED MOTEN

INTRODUCTION

"Allow Me to Re-Introduce Myself"

In the late fall of 2011, the *Today Show* came to George-town to do a story on my course on the rapper JAY-Z. The course had garnered quite a bit of national press, and correspondent Craig Melvin (on his first assignment, now one of the show's hosts) had been tasked to explore what we did in class. We discussed why a figure like JAY-Z belonged in a college curriculum, why some parents of the students were skeptical, and why it was important to parse JAY-Z's lyrics as poetry. Most of the media coverage of the class was positive, but there was also predictable pushback. Conservatives contended that the class was cover for my leftist views, while educational purists wondered about the value of such a course because it didn't fit into the traditional curriculum.

I was a grizzled veteran of such discussions since by that time I'd been teaching hip hop at the university level for fifteen years. I didn't romanticize hip hop, didn't make it a fetish of class identity or an avatar of authentic blackness. Rather, I approached the genre as a fascinating artistic and cultural expression that had a great deal to teach us about America and race and class and gender too. By now this must seem like old hat because surely there are hundreds of hip hop classes around the nation in colleges, and high schools too.

But that doesn't mean that most folks in our society are convinced that it is a good thing to study hip hop in the academy. The troubling resurgence of racism in American culture means that hip hop is in the spotlight again. Judging by the hate mail I get for grappling with race in my courses on JAY-Z, Kendrick Lamar, and Beyoncé, it is clear that discussions of hip hop are as compelling as ever. In response to this critical moment, artists like T.I., Meek Mill, and Cardi B use their considerable clout and prominent platforms to speak up about social injustice.

Teaching JAY-Z is especially satisfying for me. I have taught courses on the murdered actor and rap icon Tupac Shakur at several colleges and universities. I have enthusiastically covered the history of hip hop culture and music in detail in other courses. But teaching JAY-Z time and again through the years has been even more rewarding. It always involves a great degree of study with students about a range of issues and ideas, from class to gender, race to politics, public housing projects to blackness. JAY-Z provokes reflection on big social and moral concerns. And, of course, artistic ones too, although it becomes apparent the more I study him that he is no average bear, that he is, quite simply, a rhetorical genius whose wordplay and literary skill are nonpareil.

The more I pore over his lyrics, the more I realize that I am dealing with an extremely intelligent poet whose work matches the poets I've admired since childhood. My pastor at church used to trade lines of poetry with me from Tennyson and Hughes, Brooks and Yeats. I developed an appreciation for the epic sweep of culture that could be condensed into the poetic arts. JAY-Z is capable of doing the same; he can describe street hustling with an artistic verve that is every bit as beautiful and poignant as that of the best canon poets. His rolling or clipped cadences, his dense or simple descriptions, his slow or sped-up observations about life unfurl like a thickly knitted quilt cast over shivering bones.

I am impressed with how effortless JAY-Z makes it all seem. I have grown to appreciate just how much work goes into finding the right word, fitting in the right phrase, or making just the right allusion. He uses these skills to say that the rap game is in trouble, that racism is a persistent ill, and, most memorably, that no other rapper has enjoyed comparable longevity at the top.

There's never been a nigga this good for this long
This hood or this pop, this hot or this strong

With so many different flows, this one's for this song
The next one I switch up, this one will get bit up.

His verse is wildly eclectic. He can in one instant flaunt his own poetic virtue and the next instant portray the bitter contradictions of zealous belief.

I'm from the place where the church is the flakiest
And niggas been praying to God so long that they
   atheist.

As I've studied and taught, I've learned of Jay's great sense of humor, his sense of irony, his love for his craft. I learned how he uses words to make us feel the crushing heartbreak of a broken home.

Now, all the teachers couldn't reach me
And my momma couldn't beat me
Hard enough to match the pain of my pops not
   seein' me.

As I listened to JAY-Z I knew I needed to write a book about the major themes of his art, how he put his words together, and why they make sense the way they do. Jay's prodigious memory and his enormous cool made him that much more appealing. He is one of the few hip hop artists I've seen in concert who can bridge the aesthetic gulf between the studio and the stage. The intimacies and implications of a hip hop song are usually best heard in your headphones. It is far more difficult to catch a song's meaning when it's blurted out by a rapper onstage seeking to match the timing and tone of the sound booth.

I knew that to write about Jay meant to write about the themes he is taken with, to probe his verbal gifts, and to grapple with his growing political consciousness. His politics are sometimes subtle; sometimes just a phrase or a bar communicate so much meaning.

> *I arrived on the day Fred Hampton died*
> *Uh, real niggas just multiply.*

In the brief scope of this couplet Jay does a couple of important things. He identifies with a fallen member of the sixties-era Black Panther Party who was unjustly murdered by the Chicago police and the FBI. He also suggests that Hampton's spirit animated the birth of a revolutionary cultural figure like Jay himself.

It should be clear that JAY-Z is America at its scrappy, brash, irreverent, soulful, ingenious best. He is as transcendent a cultural icon as Frank Sinatra, as adventurous a self-made billionaire as Mark Zuckerberg, as gifted a poet as Walt Whitman. When we see JAY-Z, we glimpse the powerful silhouette of American ambition sketched against the canopy of national striving. When we hear JAY-Z, we listen to the incomparable tongue of American democracy expressed by a people too long held underfoot.

What JAY-Z thinks and believes, what he does and says, is the quintessential expression of who we are as a people and a nation.

The half-century mark for JAY-Z is here. He has become the genre's first billionaire. He reigns as an elder statesman in a field brimming with artists half his age. He continues to produce relevant rap records that make the charts. And he is charting an artistic and political response to revived racism and renewed hostility to blackness. Jay has logged thirty years as a recording artist. His ideas, and the issues he addresses, offer us plenty to consider. Masculinity and black love. Hustling and elections. Gentrification and generational wealth. Criminal justice reform and neighbor-to-neighbor carnage. Visual art and the unbearable whiteness of museum walls. Racial injustice and the impact of slavery. The virtues of psychotherapy and its racial misuse. American myths of patriotism and empire. Police brutality and the overmedication of black youth. And lots more besides.

The induction of JAY-Z as the first hip hop artist in the Songwriters Hall of Fame encourages us to explore his poetic gifts—his use of braggadocio and allusion, signifying and double entendre, metaphor and homophones, contronyms and metonyms. That signal honor and his towering stature also invite us to weigh his impact on hip hop and to consider what his brotherhood with immortal MC The Notorious B.I.G., his beef with rap legend Nas, and his complicated relationship with rap superstar Drake teach us about ourselves and about hip hop's reach and limits. Since this is JAY-Z's America, it is important to trace his influence on younger figures like basketball icon LeBron James and fallen rapper Nipsey Hussle, each of whom reflects elements of Jay's vision of hustling. It is instructive how even a few words from Jay bid us to reinterpret leaders like Al Sharpton and Martin Luther King, Jr., and to scrutinize geniuses become scoundrels like singer R. Kelly and comedian Bill Cosby.

This seems an ideal time to grapple with JAY-Z's lyrics and legacy, examine his ideas and imagination, assess his impact and importance. In 2003, Jay rapped, "Allow me to re-introduce myself," in his song "Public Service Announcement." Permit me to introduce his work and thinking to those who may not know him well. And allow me to re-introduce him to those who know him but haven't studied his art and evolution closely.

In 2012, JAY-Z founded the Made in America Festival, an annual two-day musical event held in Philadelphia over the Labor Day weekend. As curator of the festival, JAY-Z brings together acts from a broad array of musical genres, including hip hop, pop, R&B, Latin, EDM (electronic dance music), and indie, experimental, and alternative rock. "Through all the lines and things that are put in place to divide each other, all like-minded people gather together," Jay said on the promotional video for the inaugural festival. "We're more curious than ever. We create music to express ourselves . . . We're all trading off each other's culture. So no matter what lines you put . . . we're all somehow gonna find a way to come together 'cause the lines and the titles can never keep us apart. This is what we've been. To put that on display for the world is . . . just being honest. That's it, that's what it's all about. We are finally living out our creed."

The American creed has been defined by countless thinkers and activists and politicians since the beginning of the nation as a set of ideals that govern our existence— an appreciation for the individual, a thirst for equality, the demand of liberty, the quest for justice. Martin Luther King, Jr. in 1963, six years before Shawn Corey Carter was born, stood in Washington, D.C., on sacred civic ground in front of the Lincoln Memorial on the National Mall and dreamed out loud about an America that one day "will rise up and live out the true meaning of its creed: 'We hold these truths to be self-evident, that all men are created equal.'" Through all of Jay's hustling, versifying, and politicking, the American creed as King expressed it is what the self-proclaimed King of New York has in his own way sought to embody. It is the right time to gauge JAY-Z's stride toward freedom as a cultural colossus and to take measure of his profoundly American desire to rise to the top here and around the globe while never forgetting the place and people from whence he came.

In many ways, this is JAY-Z's America as much as

it is Obama's America, or Trump's America, or Martin Luther King's America, or Nancy Pelosi's America, or Maxine Waters's America, or Alexandria Ocasio-Cortez's America. JAY-Z has given this country a language to speak with, ideas to think through, and words to live by. His lyrics have shaped the self-understanding of a culture that grapples daily with racial and social justice. He is an important thinker and consequential artist, and instead of looking at hip hop or his life through the lens of, say, civil rights, or social respectability, or mainstream politics, it is time to see America through JAY-Z's eyes.

Rappers had long suggested that the music industry wasn't much different from the drug world (as Biggie put it, "If I wasn't in the rap game/I'd probably have a ki, knee-deep in the crack game"); now Jay-Z conflated Biggie's eloquent thug and Puffy's smooth executive to create the image of an utterly mercenary man who just happens to rap.

KELEFA SANNEH

As much as the hustler and hustler's mentality is a newer phenomenon in black communities, it is a much older practice in larger white American society. It particularly reflects a combined ethos of the capitalist economic structure and the mythos of the self-made man.

STEPHANY ROSE

"I'm the Definition of It"

HUSTLING

Let's begin with what even his greatest admirers may miss: JAY-Z is a prescient theorist of American history. No, he hasn't shaped our conception of the New World through prodigious research. He hasn't presented, like Voltaire, a *philosophie de l'histoire*. He hasn't floated a new interpretation about the American Revolution. Neither has he unveiled a shiny new understanding of the Civil War. But he has offered a theory of history, explored in the magnificent obsession of his art and career: hustling. Jay was at least a decade ahead of Pulitzer Prize–winning historian Walter McDougall, who contends in his 2004 book *Freedom Just Around the Corner* that hustling is the central motif of American history, the dominant measure of the American character.

Surveying the national scene, McDougall turns to

long-ago literary lights like Herman Melville, Mark Twain, and Willa Cather, and more recent writers like William Safire, to buttress his claim that Americans "are . . . prone to be hustlers." McDougall says this doesn't mean that Americans possess "a nature different or worse than other human beings," but that they have "enjoyed more opportunity to pursue their ambitions, by foul means or fair, than any other people in history." There is certainly a duality to hustling, a good and bad side determined by what form the activity takes and the moral environment in which it takes root and flourishes. On the one hand, writes McDougall, Melville was on the mark "to portray Americans as hustlers in the sense of self-promoters, scofflaws, occasional frauds, and peripatetic self-reinventers." On the other hand, hustlers flashed positive attributes as "builders, doers, go-getters, dreamers, hard workers, inventors, organizers, engineers, and a people supremely generous."

McDougall is careful to show both the glory and grief of hustling, its virtues and vices. But in my view, some of the most prominent defenders of the American self-image, be they right-wing evangelicals or gung-ho nationalists, relentlessly cast hustling as a solely positive example of our pluck and persistence. They often uncritically endorse questionable American enterprises and unjust exploits around the globe driven by imperial quests and a troubling hunger for global dominion. It is a national character trait that is applauded by its most zealous advocates. But hustling is rightly seen by its victims on foreign shores and those in our backyard as the menacing strike of Americanist ideology. Those outside the nation have felt the whip of American empire on their backs. Those closer to home have been lashed in the face by a nation that praises white hustle but despises such agency in their darker kin.

Before we can understand what JAY-Z has done to hustling, and how he has inspired two other cultural icons, we've got to understand what hustling has done to black America.

Black hustle has been scorned as long as black humanity has been despised and black intelligence has been questioned. The roots of black hustle run deep into slavery, where black labor largely existed on white demand. Black folk had limited time or space to themselves to enjoy their labor or lives. They lived literally off the books at the margins of white society. Most things they did for themselves, like getting married, were illegal, and reading was potentially deadly. Even when black folk were freed, Jim Crow brought different kinds of restrictions. Black folk were denied access to equal education, employment, and other social goods and services. Black strivers created voluntary associations of mutual support, such as social clubs and fraternal groups. They also created religious and civic organizations to uplift their less-fortunate kin.

But underground and informal networks of affiliation also thrived for ambitious citizens who were neither well educated nor financially well off. These folks struggled to survive through a range of off-the-books pursuits in the underground economy: running numbers, bootlegging liquor, fencing stolen goods, gambling, racketeering, dealing drugs, selling sex, and other illicit activities.

Black hustling was in part the effort to take hold of the American Dream that was touted to the white masses. On 2006's "Oh My God," Jay lays claim to that dream. He doesn't simply hustle, but he hustles the story of hustling, and thereby engages in a kind of meta-hustling. Jay tells a story that celebrates its own narrative as the manifestation of hustling. The song also becomes a conduit for hustling's spirit and goal. His story is at once representative and unique, both specific and universal. His blackness gives even more color to hustling's story of rising from the bottom to the top to fulfill the American Dream, and, as his name suggests, his divine destiny.

> *So if this is your first time hearing this*
> *You're about to experience someone so cold*
> *A journey seldom seen, the American dream*
> *From the bottom to the top of the globe they call me*
>   *Hov*

On 2007's "American Dreamin'," JAY-Z's narrator is frustrated that circumstances have thwarted his plans to achieve the American Dream of material rewards through a college education. In the narrator's case, and that of his peers, their dreams are realized through hustling because school isn't an option, times are urgent, and food and other resources are scarce.

> *This is the shit you dream about*
> *With the homies steaming out*
> *Back-to-back, backing them Bimmers out*
> *Seems as our plans to get a grant*
> *Then go off to college, didn't pan or even out*
> *. . .*
> *Mama forgive me, should be thinking about*
> * Harvard*
> *But that's too far away, niggas are starving*

As with Jay's hustler, black folks' lives have been shaped by restrictions on social mobility, economic prosperity, employment opportunities, and housing prospects. Some black folk managed to thrive despite these restrictions because of superior networks of support and encouragement. In the late nineteenth and early twentieth centuries black folk built strong black businesses and stable black schools in all-black neighborhoods. Those who fell between the cracks, like Jay's narrator in present-day America, were often left to fend for themselves. It was difficult enough for stable or well-to-do black people to survive in a culture that oppressed black folk at every turn. It was virtually impossible for blacks without formal education or social standing to make it without helping themselves in the underground economy.

The brutal class bifurcation between the black thrivers and the black thrashed persists to this day. Big forces loom that punish the black poor. There are broad shifts in the economy away from manufacturing. There are the rise of the knowledge economy and the proliferation of automated technologies that displace human labor. There is the expansion of service industries that call for extensive retraining. And there is the vast re-segregation of public schools. These conditions make the underground inescapable, the best among bad options.

Black hustle has at least three meanings. First, it describes a plight and condition. Like Immanuel Kant's *Ding an sich*, it is the thing-in-itself, the game, the hustle. (As Jay said, "You can't knock the hustle," and when he said it in 1996, his hustle was rapping, and his "job" was selling drugs.) Second, it expresses, as a verb, an activity, the performance of a hustle. Third, as a noun, it names the person who is the hustler. The hustle, the plight, the condition, is what black folk are caught in when their resources are depleted, their access to legitimate goods severely restricted, their ability to enjoy social and educational equality greatly curtailed. The hustle is the main resort for those who are systematically deprived of benefits and advantages in society. The hustle beckons those who are excluded from privilege and power. Hustling, the action, the performance, is embraced because it often provides the only relief from economic misery. The hustler is determined not to suffer silently and turns distress to opportunity.

On 1999's "Dope Man," Jay's frail narrator indicts a racist society for destroying black dreams of education and professional success. He also accuses society of flooding black neighborhoods with drugs, thus leaving him and his peers little choice but to hustle.

> *A-hem, I'm a prisoner of circumstance*
> *Frail nigga, I couldn't much work with my hands*
> *But my mind was strong, I grew where you hold*
>   *your blacks up*
> *Trap us, expect us not to pick gats up*
> *Where you drop your cracks off by the Mack trucks*
> *Destroy our dreams of lawyers and actors*
> *Keep us spiralin', goin' backwards*

Like Jay's narrator on "Dope Man," poor black youth routinely confront enormous odds. Poor chances at a good education and a good job leave them in grave peril. Social scientists such as Tatiana Adeline Thieme say that young folk in places like the Middle East and Africa who face similar conditions are caught in a version of "waithood" between childhood and adulthood. "Waithood" is a period of artificially prolonged adolescence.

The economic and social forces that stagnate progress

force some of the youth into the underground economy. The tragedy is that too often this isn't the exception but the rule for American black youth. They are denied opportunities that would propel them into stable adulthood. They are often seen as less worthy of support in the achievement of milestones set for other youth. There is, instead, for many black youth, a "weighthood": heavy economic and social burdens weigh on their shoulders and keep them from rising.

Their condition is exacerbated by another factor: studies show that black youth are often perceived as older than they are, that adolescents are perceived as adults. They are subject to harsher treatment for misbehavior and perceived social offenses, and suffer consequences usually reserved for adults. Thus, while their progress is delayed, American black youth are abruptly rushed into adulthood without support or nurture. They are often hemmed in by a society that seeks to crush them, an underground that exposes them to high risk, and a culture that disdains their blackness. Black youth get involved in the hustle out of necessity. They hustle to stay alive, and the hustlers among them are both reviled and revered. They are, in essence, acrobats of competing liminalities. They swing among rival transitional existences in schools that don't cherish them, justice systems that stigmatize them, and underground cultures that may end up killing them.

Positive, legitimate, legal black hustling can be termed *bright* hustling. It encompasses a wide range of activities:

creating multiple streams of income, renting a room in your house, earning passive income through real estate investments, opening a small business, building banks, donating blood for money, coming up with a computer software app for mobile devices, getting a Ph.D., playing professional sports, becoming a lawyer, doctor, engineer, hairdresser, barber, factory worker or accountant, and just doing everything in one's power to get ahead. It rests on the intellectual efforts that have the best chance of being cherished and celebrated, and which thrive in the well-lit arenas of wholesome cultural enterprise. There is of course no assurance that such efforts will be supported in the mainstream. Black folk have always had to defend their right to be go-getters. Even legal hustling has often been viewed as intrinsically troubling.

For a long spell, especially under Jim Crow, bright hustling was seen as disruptive to white society. Bright hustling often thrived as a valiant complaint against social injustice, since whites made every effort to shut it down. In fact, bright hustling was often viewed as no better than criminal behavior. Black folk with drive and ambition were viewed as uppity and disrespectful. They were made to feel guilty for striving after honest work and valid rewards. Their industry was viewed as that of the bandit. Bright hustlers were seen as moral renegades and lawbreaking anarchists. The notion that black folk could create their own businesses and make their way in the world because of brains angered white folk to no end.

Legitimate black striving may as well have been illegal activity. White society sought to outlaw black prosperity as much as possible, and where the law couldn't work, then violence came into play. The remarkable show of black entrepreneurship in Tulsa, Oklahoma, in 1921, in an area dubbed "Black Wall Street," provoked extraordinary white vengeance. White mobs used guns, incendiary devices, explosives, and airplanes to destroy what was then the nation's wealthiest black community.

The illegal, illicit, underground dimensions of black hustling can be termed *blight* hustling. Besides the off-the-books underground activities cited above, it includes far less offensive illegal enterprises like selling "loosies" (single cigarettes) from packs without tax stamps, an activity that led to Eric Garner's tragic death by cops in New York City in 2014, or selling bootleg music and movies, as Alton Sterling did in 2016 outside a Baton Rouge store before he suffered the same fate as Garner. It is the kind of hustling carried on at the corners of the culture when other avenues are roadblocked.

In between bright and blight hustling lies *site* hustling, which names a far more ambiguous state of affairs. Site hustling uses locales—the street, the abandoned apartment, the garbage dump, the lawn—as the scenes of everyday struggles for survival. It is at these sites, among others, where folk, for instance, collect discarded bottles and cans or steel and iron for money. It is where they find temporary shelter. It is where they gather the remnants of discarded food. Or it is where they cut grass or lay sod for wages that are not reported. All of this happens off the grid and beyond formal work. It occurs in a make-do, soft, underground economy that is informal but certainly not dramatically illegal. Site hustlers often face persistent precarity in the face of unreliable resources.

JAY-Z's hustling is a two-pronged affair. First, Jay raps about his former days as a hustler, making his former illicit activity, and the ill-gotten gains from his illegal enterprise, the subject of his present hustle. If the Supreme Court can declare that corporations are people and money is speech, then Jay is right to demand that, "We can talk, but money talks, so talk mo' bucks," in recognition that

> *I'm not a businessman; I'm a business, man!*
> *Let me handle my business, damn.*

That is the Hustler's Credo in a cunning couplet.

Second, Jay has fully transitioned from underground to aboveground economies, and thus has redeemed hustling as a positive behavior for himself and others like him. Jay in his bright hustling mode has not only turned repeatedly to hustling for artistic inspiration. He has also served as a gifted interpreter of blight hustling's harsh necessities. He has argued that such hustling can't help but occur in a country that sees its dark citizens as disposable. But he has been careful also to lament the fatal downside of hustling. He has often expressed an ambivalence about the hustling life, spoken of the regrets one has to live with in order to survive. On 1996's "Regrets," Jay's narrator says:

> *Coppers was watchin' us through nighttime*
> *binoculars*
> . . .
> *Make me wanna holler back at the crib in the sauna*
> *Prayin' my people bailed out like TimeWarner*
> *Awaitin' a call, from his kin, not the coroner*
> *Phone in my hand, nervous confined to a corner*
> *Beads of sweat, second thoughts on my mind*
> *How can I ease the stress and learn to live with these*
> *regrets?*

Beginning on his first album, Jay offered crucial insight about blight hustling's raison d'être. "Well, we hustle out of a sense of hopelessness," he announces on the spoken intro to "Can I Live," before reciting his verse. "Sort of a desperation. Through that desperation, we become addicted. Sort of like the fiends we accustomed to servin'." Time and again Jay establishes, between those who sell coke and those who smoke it, a bittersweet communion in their symbiotic addictions. This unites those who are the merchants of crystallized death and those whose addictive consumption of crack crystallized an entire generation's social death. What social critic Mike Davis in his book *City of Quartz* calls "the political economy of crack" not only afforded opportunities for drug dealers and other hustlers, but it increased community social disorder and chaos in its wake. Hustling both fueled and fed off the hopelessness of ghettoes across the country. It is that hopeless condition that led Jay to sell cocaine "til brains was fried to a fricassee." It kept him from worrying over the loss of human capital or life. But he finally grappled with the cost of his hustle in the redeeming retrospect that art offers.

> *Can't lie, at the time it never bothered me*
> *At the bar, gettin' my thug on properly*
> *My squad and me, lack of respect for authority*
> *Laughin' hard, happy to be escapin' poverty,*
>   *however brief.*

The "however brief" coda underscores just how notions of the precarious and the sporadic gang up to deliver a blow both to the dealer and to those to whom the drugs are dealt. Jay was a once and future retailer of the first order, first in selling crack, and next in telling the story of what he and so many others felt they were compelled by circumstance to do. Not to glamorize blight hustling, but to explicitly discourage its expression by artistically exploring its dangers and seductions and its lethal consequences. In this case, it's better to tell, not show, which is a way to diminish harm by speaking of it rather than doing it. Jay efficiently captures this idea in his 2001 song "Izzo (H.O.V.A.)," where he substitutes the selling of drugs with telling us about his having sold drugs while warning his listeners not to do it. We witness him go from street entrepreneur to grassroots ethnographer, from blight hustler to bright hustler.

> *Hov is back, life stories told through rap*
> *Niggas acting like I sold you crack*
> *Like I told you sell drugs, no, Hov did that*
> *So hopefully you won't have to go through that.*

Perhaps the biggest benefit of reading McDougall and listening to JAY-Z in tandem is the language they give us to battle the mammoth badness of one of the greatest hucksters, swindlers, and debilitating liars the country has known. A man who, since his election in 2016, has let flow a stream of moral obscenity and spiritual belligerence that has polluted the wells of our democracy. The heinous hustler has unleashed fearsome waves of fascism in nearly uninterrupted spasms of political insanity.

It is not he alone who is at fault. It is not just his solipsistic worldview and isolationist politics that threaten us. It is the maddening complicity of men and women who know better. They compound their sin through defiant amnesia. They try to make us forget that they deemed the forty-fourth occupant of the Oval Office a Black

Monster. An irrevocable noncitizen. An irreversible alien. An indisputable nonhuman who ruined this country because he was unforgivably black. Meanwhile, the white shivering class—those who are politically and morally spooked by "otherness"—has been badly hoodwinked. In the bargain basement of retail politics they got hustled into believing the most self-aggrandizing blowhard in American political history was the right man for the job. McDougall says that in Herman Melville's arguably greatest novel, *The Confidence-Man*,

> *Melville took the risk of telling the truth, as he saw it, about the tricks Americans played on themselves in their effort to worship both God and Mammon. His Confidence-Man, variously likened to a jester, traveling salesman, "genial misanthrope," P.T. Barnum (who published his scandalous autobiography in 1855), the Devil, an angel, and the Second Coming of Christ, is a master of disguise and persuasion. Though some passengers* [aboard a Mississippi steamboat that is the setting for the novel] *prove tougher to gull than others, he eventually employs their own fear, greed, or fancied virtue to pry open their wallets, exposing in the process every conundrum and lie—about slavery, Indians, business, industry, and frontier religion—Americans preferred not to acknowledge.*

America's Heartless Hustler has surely turned the suspicion of the myriad "others" in our culture to his crooked advantage. He has lied about himself to inflate his importance and lied about others to diminish theirs. His cruelly multiplied mendacities have choked trust and stoked fear. He repeatedly claims in stark delusion to be one of our greatest truth tellers. He has pried open the purse strings of his blinkered adherents and separated them from their votes. As McDougall says of Melville's character, the "Con-Man does not persecute them so much as assist their self-flagellation: he is accuser, prosecutor, judge, bailiff, and even redeemer insofar as the dupes can blame their misfortune on the *Con-Man's* bad faith. Can no one resist? Are none sufficiently holy or cynical to escape the urge to prove they are what they're not?"

Not to be outdone by a fraudulent miscarriage of bright hustling, Jay told David Letterman in 2018 that Donald Trump is "actually a great thing" because he is "forcing people to . . . have a conversation and band together and work together." Jay argued that one "can't really address something that's not revealed," and that Trump "is bringing out an ugly side of America that we wanted to believe was gone . . . We still gotta deal with it. We have to have tough conversations—talk about the N-word, talk about why white men are so privileged in this country."

Trump's bristling contempt for blackness and people of color around the world spilled over as he targeted Haiti, El

Salvador, and several African countries, asking in a meeting with senators in January 2018, "Why are we having all these people from shithole countries come here?" JAY-Z cleverly responded to Trump's bile on CNN later that month.

> It's disappointing and hurtful . . . But this has been going on. This is how people talk behind closed doors . . . Because once you [drive racists into hiding], all the other closet racists just run back into the hole. You haven't fixed anything. What you've done is spray perfume on a trash can. And when you do that . . . you create a superbug, because you don't take care of the problem. You don't take the trash out, you just keep spraying whatever over it to make it acceptable. And then as those things grow, you create a superbug. And now we have Donald Trump, the superbug.

That's a bright hustler speaking to a bigoted one.

No matter what we think of JAY-Z's magnificent obsession with hustling, there is little doubt that he has willed himself, by dint of his talent, to change from a man who sowed mayhem in his urban community to a man who gives nobler meaning to hustling. For him hustling is inspired by loving your own, rescuing and sticking up for the poor members of the hood he no longer has to live in. It means grappling with the vicious forces of white supremacy and black self-destruction. Hopefully the true hustler's microphone will amplify love long after the tragic trickster has been forced from the limelight and has climbed down for the last time from his bully pulpit.

In a fashion, hustle play in basketball—diving after loose balls, working hard to win—mirrors hustling in the broader culture: it's valued off the box score, is important to the game, and can gain you extra possessions. There are few professional players who have hustled harder than LeBron James. He is not only a player of extraordinary athletic ability, but, above all, a basketball savant with a genius intelligence quotient who plays the game from the neck up and not merely from the shoulders down. He has risen from dire economic circumstances in a hardscrabble existence in Ohio to become a world-class athlete, parlaying his talent on the court to ingenious business moves off the court. He also uses his financial independence in the fight for black freedom, whether by openly addressing persistent racism or speaking bluntly about the bigotry of many white Americans.

It is a splendid fate that JAY-Z and LeBron teamed up for several charitable dinners in the mid- to late 2000s during the annual NBA All-Star weekend under the banner of "Two Kings," well after LeBron had begun to see Jay as a mentor. Their royal pairing showed the synergy of two cultural juggernauts who amplify the vitality of music and games the world over. That two figures who have gone from being seen as occasional pariahs—one as an iconic rapper who nevertheless courted suspicion because of a drug-dealing past, the other as a superstar athlete who has shaken up the league by defying convention and precedent—to being viewed as indispensable participants in song and sports is a tribute to the culture that produced them and gave them the chutzpah to believe they could do it at all. JAY-Z and LeBron have approached the art of the boardroom deal and the management of image and brand with as much panache as they have shown on stage and court.

For JAY-Z that includes venturing into a clothing line, footwear, a cologne, an entertainment club, alcohol brands, a record label, an entertainment company that includes artist and athlete management as well as a television and film division, and a music streaming service. For LeBron that includes an endorsement portfolio with major national sports, beverage, food, and automotive brands; a production company; a media company; a stake in a British soccer team; the LeBron James Family Foundation; and his enormously successful I Promise School in Akron, Ohio. Much of this grew from his partnership with a longtime friend, businessman and media personality Maverick Carter.

The urge to secure their bases with trusted figures may explain why JAY-Z keeps friends from his childhood and blight hustling days in a close circle and why LeBron brings along folk from his past, like Carter, and provides them with opportunities to shine and explore their talent in ways they'd never otherwise enjoy. Soon after his first championship run with the Miami Heat, LeBron left agent Leon Rose and entrusted his basketball future to another longtime friend, Rich Paul. LeBron, like his mentor JAY-Z, was sending a signal that black intelligence should be supported just as black loyalty should be rewarded. Those gestures are every bit as political as LeBron and his mates in 2012 tweeting out a picture of themselves garbed in hoodies in solidarity with the murdered youth Trayvon Martin.

Hip hop and sports stars inspire each other because both have often overcome odds through hard work and talent. Their common efforts to achieve reflect both the heart of the American Dream and the core of hustling in the eyes of Melville. Of course, legendary coach and infamous curmudgeon Phil Jackson may have had a racially troubled view of hustling in mind, one that reinforces the perception of bright hustling ruffling the feathers of the white establishment, when he denigrated and demoted LeBron's business partners by referring to them as his "posse."

Jay and LeBron have both used their cultural capital to enliven our definition of hustling by broadening their base and extending their influence and visibility—and their power. For instance, JAY-Z and his wife were greeted as royalty by a fawning citizenry at President Obama's second inauguration, and a week later, LeBron sent Instagrams from the White House. Without either man engaging in visible protest or the most obvious forms of social resistance, LeBron and his mentor JAY-Z are bringing a new definition of black masculine identity and achievement to the public realm. It grants them access to Frank Sinatra–level autonomy and Barack Obama–level audacity, without forcing them to give up the hustling ethic that unites hip hop and black versions of basketball.

The transformative interaction of art and athletics, of hip hop and hoops, offers a powerful antidote to the exploitation of black athletes and entertainers. JAY-Z and LeBron have helped to facilitate a remarkable transformation beyond their own stage and court: a new generation of ballers and rappers are redefining success with a black twist as they polish their brands and expand their market reach. This is more than wealth creation. It is the politics of social justice injected into sports and entertainment. It is about creating opportunities for black enterprise and opening doors for other black folk—a crucial goal of black politics and protest. JAY-Z and LeBron are proxies of a persistent push for black progress. They embody the reversal of the paradigm of white agents, executives, and accountants ripping off black figures and reducing their economic efficacy and, therefore, their political power. When LeBron fires white folk and hires black folk, it is not reverse racism, nor merely a reversal of racially unjust

patterns of business. It is the fruitful outcome of the opportunity given to black talent. It is a proud and effective
affirmation of black excellence. It is bright hustling at its
best.

There is little illusion, however, that their success off-
sets the vicious blowback to black progress. Nor does it
singlehandedly counter deeply rooted racial injustice. To
be sure, the bulk of poor black folk remain trapped in
circumstances where poverty, social dislocation, shrink-
ing government welfare, gang warfare, and other forms
of chaotic violence persist. The heroic achievement of hip
hop and athletic stars alike—and the reason their arcs of
emergence and escape are similarly celebrated—is public
recognition for their talent. And the recognition of their
talent leads to a recognition of black talent in other arenas. Those who are in a position to hustle, to climb and
strive because of education, find hope and inspiration to
excel in their realms of pursuit because of LeBron and
Jay's narratives of success. Those who are left behind in
poor neighborhoods project their desires and pin their
hopes on those who escape.

Inside and outside black hoods across America, a potent
narrative has formed that argues there are only three ways
out of the ghetto: hustling, hip hop, and hoops. JAY-Z's
narrator on 2002's "Some How Some Way" acknowledges
this holy trinity of escape routes while throwing in comedy
to boot. He also gives a nod to the earnest labor of the

working class while desperately wishing to leave the dangerous life of hustling behind.

> *Whether we dribble out this motherfucker*
> *Rap metaphors and riddle out this motherfucker*
> *Work second floors, hospital out this motherfucker*
> *Some how we gotta get up out this motherfucker*
> *Some day the cops'll kill a muh' fucker*
> *I don't always wanna be this drug dealing*
> *   muh' fucker, damn*

And even though one comes from hoops and the other from hip hop, LeBron's and JAY-Z's careers reveal a sublime convergence. They show the best way out of the ghetto is to use God-given talent and heroic hustle to relentlessly fight the inequality that holds back so many black folk.

Of course, when prominent blacks hustle hard to take hold of that dream and exercise their rights and privileges, the broader culture doesn't always accept it. Barack Obama studied hard, went to Harvard, and became president, and yet that hard-won achievement remained a sore spot for the millions who refused to see him as American and the politicians who blocked his legislation. Not everyone wanted to bolster his agenda to reach all segments of society. When, nearly ten years ago, LeBron sought to exercise his right to free agency like so many have done before him, he encountered ill will and strong resistance. King James was dethroned in the hearts of millions and became the NBA's bête noire after divorcing the Cleveland Cavaliers and pledging his free-agent love to the Miami Heat. His sin was forgetting that he couldn't fire owners who reserved the right to fire players. Yet today he stands astride far more than the sports world, as his corporate interests and endorsement deals prove.

But the resistance to LeBron wasn't exclusively about his controversial method of departure, in which the ballplayer chose to announce his leaving Cleveland for Miami in a nationally televised special, "The Decision," that raised $6 million for charity. LeBron was hung in effigy and exposed to the racial animus of thwarted fans in Cleveland, which proved how shallow the love was to begin with. That response reflected an experience common to other black stars, who know that once they exceed expectations, or transgress norms or limits or boundaries in a way that few other blacks before them have done, there is hell to pay. When the Miami Heat darkened the White House to celebrate their first championship, King James and President Obama may have had more to discuss than their love for ball and hip hop.

The history of black struggle against the odds, the legacy of black hustling to soar above limits, suggests that the same black culture that is perceived by some as portending trouble and provokes their ire will eventually find its rhythm of acceptance in the broad arena of American society. This arc will play out in athletic and pop cultures before politics. That is why there was a Jackie Robinson before there was a Martin Luther King, Jr., a JAY-Z before there was a Barack Obama. (Of course, sometimes the road to betterment is winding, the struggle protracted, the progress delayed. As the political arc of Muhammad Ali suggests, Colin Kaepernick, now an outcast in professional football for taking a stand against police brutality and racial oppression, may very well be widely celebrated one day for his heroic resistance.)

Remarkably, the Two Kings iteration of the hustle and dream of equality—*You are not going to tell me how to be me, and I have the cash, the credibility, and the talent to make sure I do it my way with your children's blessing*—has found broad acceptance in American society. Past pioneers of black style and swag paid a heavy price so that today's bright hustlers could enjoy the fruits of their labor. There would be no tattooed LeBron James, whose body art and style may be a source of curiosity but not outright revulsion, without Allen Iverson, who pioneered body art and style. And the lineage stretches back to 2Pac, whose inked body narrated the truths of his existence and inspired Iverson. When Iverson came into the NBA more than twenty years ago, he was considered a menace and a thug because of his cornrows and the tattoos that were famously airbrushed from his body when he appeared on the cover of the NBA's *Hoop* magazine. Those tattoos are no longer seen as the province of thugs but as creative self-expression.

When in 2005 NBA commissioner David Stern imposed a dress code that took aim at the most obvious signifiers of hip hop culture, including sagging pants, large jewelry, Timberlands, and do-rags, it was perceived by critics as a thinly veiled attempt to suppress the growing influence of black culture. But by then, basketball's biggest stars, including LeBron, had moved on to more prestigious designer brands. Again, they took their inspiration from rappers like JAY-Z, who would "Change Clothes," as one of his songs about maturing suggested, moving from the recording studio to the boardroom. While few were looking, something profound was brewing: the hip hopper and baller became *America's* new superstars, and no dress codes, social obstacles, stylistic aversions, or racial barriers could keep them down. Dress code or no, NBA stars wove their styles into the fabric of American culture one stitch at a time, using catchy eyewear and flamboyant colors to align themselves with the brash and independent artistry of rappers.

Hip hop artists enjoy the freedom to say in their music things that many athletes wish they could say. No one has captured the spirit of ball and response more than JAY-Z, redefining swagger as he brags on his recording "Public Service Announcement":

I got a hustler spirit, nigga, period
Check out my hat yo, peep the way I wear it
Check out my swag' yo, I walk like a ballplayer
No matter where you go, you are what you are player.

Rappers want to be ballers; JAY-Z frequently refers to himself in the same breath as Michael Jordan and LeBron James. Ballers want to be rappers; the athlete-rapper moniker runs from Shaquille O'Neal and Iman Shumpert to Damian "Dame D.O.L.L.A." Lillard. JAY-Z has mastered both realms: he is a world-class rapper with a sports agency and has iconic status in professional basketball. He has also infused rap and basketball with the charismatic ghetto swag that has taken him from the Marcy Projects to Barclays Center.

Perhaps JAY-Z's and LeBron's most important contribution lies beyond the gilded fields of performance they have both ingeniously explored. The civil rights generation, and even the Michael Jordan generation, had to convince the mainstream that they were worthy of acceptance through appropriate dress and diction. JAY-Z and LeBron have, in contrast, embraced Ralph Waldo Emerson's dictum: "To be yourself in a world that is constantly trying to make you something else is the greatest accomplishment." And they've taken it further: if you are better than the best and build a compelling brand, the world will beat a path to your door and you can dress and speak any damn way you please. Or as JAY-Z put it: "Ball so hard muhfuckas wanna fine me / But first niggas gotta find me."

If JAY-Z's mentorship in hustling inspired LeBron, it also encouraged another figure who, like Jay, hustled in the streets before he turned his talents to the microphone. Like LeBron, this person had an impoverished upbringing and faced equally tough choices in the hood; unlike LeBron, his story ended violently on the very streets on which he had once hustled. The titanic wave of grief let loose by rapper and entrepreneur Nipsey Hussle's grotesque murder in March 2019 on the street outside his Los Angeles clothing store was at once astonishing and completely understandable. He was, to be sure, a gifted artist who had put out a slew of mixtapes for a decade. But he had only recently emerged on the national scene in 2018 with *Victory Lap*, his first major-label album. He was deeply loved in Los Angeles because he was profoundly committed to his neighborhood, to its economic revitalization, its physical restoration, its moral and social uplift—and to tapping its long-ignored geographical advantages. His commitment was so ironclad that he was christened "Neighborhood Nip." The massive mourning around the country in the wake of his death testified to the deep nerve he struck in the nation's conscience. His selfless gestures were more than charity, more than animated altruism; they were, instead, the passionate devotion of a man out for justice for his people.

Among the most sorely aggrieved was JAY-Z, who had supported Nipsey's early entrepreneurial exploits, his bright hustling, when he purchased, for $100 each, 100 copies of Hussle's independently released 2013 mixtape *Crenshaw*. Jay eventually mentored Nipsey and applauded his desire to remain rooted in his community. Still, like many others, Jay anguished over the cruel paradox of Nipsey's death: that he perished in the hood he refused to leave because he wanted to provide a promising future for just the sort of man who eventually took his life.

> *I never dreamed that he get killed in the place that*
> *he called home*
> *How we gonna get in power if we kill the source?*

Nearly a month after Nipsey's shocking slaughter, Jay spat those words at New York's Webster Hall in a somber soliloquy as the music halted and his voice rang across the iconic venue.

> *I be going to sleep hoping Nip visit me*
> *That young king had a lot of jewels to split with me.*

Nipsey possessed many jewels of wisdom indeed. Viewing video recordings of Jay's already legendary freestyle for Nipsey brought to mind a line of lamentation from Hussle's final single: "How you die thirty somethin' after banging all them years?" Nipsey posed that question about a fallen colleague on a song released about a month before he met a similar fate. The ex-gangbanger Hussle said he took to the "sauna sheddin' tears / All this money, power, fame and I can't make you reappear."

Yet Nipsey, although absent in body, is present in spirit more than ever. How does a rapper who was just coming into his own fill the Staples Center for his funeral and cast a spell over a society that barely knew his name the day he died? When news of Nipsey's death spread, it shook us because his lanky 6-foot, 4-inch frame carried the hopes and aspirations of his community and, we soon discovered, of so many more communities like his across the country. His accent was distinctly black American. His face, unquestionably African. The ink on his body was rooted in part in gang culture. The style of his everyday dress was unapologetically urban. And yet he touched folk far beyond his native soil and society.

One reason Hussle's death gripped the collective imagination is because his story fit into competing narratives across an ideological spectrum. While some folk advocate pulling yourself up by your bootstraps, he showed that he believed in hustling and hard work and black uplift and self-reliance and he started several businesses in the hood. He may as well have been Booker T. Washington in a baseball cap. While some folk are motivated to fight the powers that be, Nipsey believed in a politics of justice for the oppressed and poor. He joined fellow rapper YG on a song indicting Donald Trump: "I'm from a place where you prolly can't go / Speakin' for some people that you prolly ain't know."

But the main reason his story is so compelling is because love was at the core of his beliefs and behavior. Love of his craft. Love of his blackness. Love of his neighborhood. Love of his partner, the actress Lauren London, and of their children. In Instagram posts and other social media outlets, and in a 2019 spread in *GQ* magazine, the couple cemented their reputation as hood royalty and a younger generation's version of JAY-Z and Beyoncé. And, belatedly, across the nation, in vigils and outpourings of unashamed adoration, the nation showed its love of Hussle for loving so faithfully while few of us knew or paid attention. His death is even more haunting because the love he showed took place against the backdrop of unsettling violence, both real and artistically imagined, both in structural forces and intimate spaces, often conjured or measured by his own pen.

Hussle captured both his métier and his pedigree when he dubbed himself on his song "Dedication" the "2Pac of my generation," a clear-eyed if fatal prophecy. There are certainly differences. Tupac's resonant baritone, steeped in the sonic registers of the East and West coasts where he came of age, echoed eerily across the artistic and social landscape and garnered him global fame before death made him a transcendent icon. Nipsey's voice drawled in a Southern cadence inflected with California bravado that produced a *Louisiangeles* accent. Death greatly amplified that sound. Both Pac and Nip were transformed in death from hood griots to ghetto saints, from verbal magicians to generational martyrs.

Like Pac, Nip was a restless creator of rhymes, foraging through his welter of experiences, and those of his peers, to mine narrative gold in a relentless series of mixtapes. On the tragically prescient *Bullets Ain't Got No Name, Vol. 1,* he probes, like many before him, South Central LA's underground political economy, with its attendant street carnage. Nipsey's contribution is a clever deconstruction of the Blood/Crip binary by noting that Crips bang on Crips while Bloods take out Bloods. On *The Marathon*, arguably his best effort next to *Victory Lap*, Nip feels less compelled to establish what hood he's from. That neighborhood was Slauson, which he settled on his first mixtape, *Slauson Boy Vol. 1.* It figures in Nipsey's canon as his answer to legendary hip hop debuts like Nas's *Illmatic* or JAY-Z's *Reasonable Doubt.* His violent calling card of banging and slanging is clear. And yet in *The Marathon* he articulates a politics of possibility that crystalizes in the figure of the marathon.

The marathon trope found repeated use and now looms as Nipsey's legacy hashtag: the long haul of life, with planning for the future, something so many of his peers were denied or felt was impossible to achieve. On

Nip Hussle the Great Vol. 2, Nipsey eloquently explores a theme that resounded loudly, brutally, in bitter irony, after his death: that hustling and "coming up" in the hood breeds seething jealousy and paralyzing envy. Nip brags, in a luminous line of vernacular poetry, that he "turns innocence into militance," while lesser, more hateful peers are turned into murderous zealots. On *Crenshaw*, Nip propagates, as a homegrown anthropologist of sorts, a holistic hoodism, a complicated, nuanced, colorful view of the neighborhood through the eyes of one of its most prolific partisans. "Broke niggas die slow / while the rich get richer," he observes.

All of his mixtapes have been rhetorical legs along a marathon of building expression—the lyrical speeds vary, the cadences dip and swerve, the flows change pace and purpose. Nip was right to take a bow to the end of one phase of his career and welcome the beginning of another: running in the mainstream, his verbal arms swiping at the air around him, his literary feet kicking high behind him, his artistic eyes on the mark of his high calling before him. "I'm prolific, so gifted / I'm the type that's gon go get it, no kiddin'," an ode to a Melvillean view of hustling for sure. Just as JAY-Z has done, Nip constantly combated anti-intellectualism. "They tell me, 'Hussle dumb it down, you might confuse 'em.'" He refused. "Know he a genius, he just can't claim it / 'Cause they left him no platform to explain it." Hussle garnered a Grammy nomination for *Victory Lap* and seemed poised to be recognized as one of the most important figures in hip hop, or, as he rapped it, "the street's voice out west."

He loved his craft, and he used it to talk about how much he loved his neighborhood too. While others poured stigma on his community, he showered love on Slauson Avenue, on Crenshaw Boulevard, located in the heart of the Crenshaw district in South Los Angeles, redeeming these demonized geographies often left to their own devices. He didn't just represent them in song, as important as that was, but he offered the hood a green economy—as in dollar bills—and opened business doors that had been closed to neighborhood citizens. (The burger joint that formerly forbade young black folk from "loitering" on its premises had to pay rent to Nipsey when he bought the Crenshaw strip mall it was housed in.) He turned hustling to hope, destruction to dreams, and banging to bucks. He fed, clothed, and housed in his businesses the aspirations of a neighborhood.

Nipsey loved and embraced his blackness, a blackness that was bigger than the sum of its intriguing parts. He was every bit the unapologetic patron of South Central Los Angeles, with odes to hustling, banging, and higher aspirations too. But when he was eighteen he traveled to Eritrea to embrace his East African roots in his father's homeland. In 2018, Nipsey, his brother, and his father made another pilgrimage to their Eritrean Motherland to learn more from their proud soil of blackness. The voyage gave Nipsey renewed inspiration for his reverse-gentrification Husslenomics: Own your master record-ings, master your own entrepreneurial terrain, recycle capital in the hood by reinvesting earnings back into the people and places that inspired your art.

There is broad discussion about the futility of narrow views of blackness and the need to emphasize the trans-atlantic routes of black identity. Nipsey embodied the crisscrossing and crosscutting ways of global blackness and the awareness that no one culture or country or tribe has ownership of a blissfully variegated blackness. It was that sense of blackness that linked a scholar like me and a rapper like him when we shared a five-hour flight in 2018 from Los Angeles to New York. "Are you Michael Eric Dyson?" he asked as he slid into the seat next to me. "I read your books." "Yes, sir. Are you Nipsey Hussle?" I replied as I showed him that I had downloaded his latest album on my smartphone. "I listen to your music." We both smiled. We had an epic conversation. He brought up the psychologist Abraham Maslow, and we discussed Hussle's journey from gangbanging to hip hop, and espe-cially our unblushing love for black culture.

Nipsey's murder reveals a darker side of blackness: The revelation that the man charged with killing Nipsey is named Eric Holder, the same as the first black United States attorney general, is an unavoidable metaphor of the destructive doppelganger that often lurks in black life. That for all the effort to do well and be right, there are opposing forces that seek to subvert, distract, and destroy. Nipsey was a more delightful doppelganger, borrowing his nom de plume from Nipsey Russell, the black comedian known as the poet laureate of television whose comedy reveled in aphorism and rhymes.

Nipsey's demise has caused some to rally anew against black-on-black violence or to argue that staying in the hood is the problem, that one should pull up stakes. Both arguments merit consideration. Black-on-black crime is best seen as a problem of proximity, not pigment. A disturbing number of those who live in deprived communities without resource or option may indeed wreak havoc. But the same was true for white ethnics who lived in ghettoes in the late nineteenth and early twentieth centuries. As Harvard professor Khalil Muhammad argues in *The New York Times*, at the turn of the century, white figures like Harvard economist William Ripley and prominent social worker Jane Addams worked hard to rescue poor white communities plagued by violence from being further victimized by stigma, isolation, and fear. As white youth gang-related gun violence spiked, Addams "insisted that everyone from the elite to community organizers to police officers had a part to play." Muhammad says that white progressives "mobilized institutional resources to save killers and the future victims of killers," flooded violent white neighborhoods "with social workers, police reformers, and labor activists committed to creating better jobs and building a social welfare net," and then, predictably, white-on-white violence "fell slowly but steadily in proportion to economic development and crime prevention."

Black folk were treated quite differently. Black crime and violence evoked no compassion from white progressives but instead, as Muhammad argues, reinforced racist beliefs that black folk were their "own worst enemies." This led to the criminalization of black people "through various institutions and practices, whether Southern chain gangs, prison farms, convict lease camps and lynching bees or Northern anti-black neighborhood violence and race riots." The criminalization of black folk carries into the present; black people are seen, Muhammad says, as "dangerous, legitimizing or excusing white-on-black violence, conflating crime and poverty with blackness, and perpetuating punitive notions of 'justice'—vigilante violence, stop-and-frisk racial profiling and mass incarceration—as the only legitimate responses."

Of course, explaining that neighborhood more than color shapes crime doesn't relieve the horrors of black-on-black carnage. After citing studies that show that between 1989 and 1994 more black men were murdered in America than lost their lives during the Vietnam War, JAY-Z, in his memoir *Decoded*, says that the nation "did not want to talk about the human damage, or the deeper causes of the carnage." But then the American nightmare of black violence—and the blunt insistence that it was caused in large measure by the neglect of black communities—came to life in rap in the late seventies.

Rap music forced the country to confront its ugly denial and see clearly the costs of its racist legacy. Jay says that the "volume and urgency [of hardcore rap] kept a story alive that a lot of people would have preferred to disappear." Yet it must be acknowledged that anti-black animus haunts black psyches too, and the self-hatred, and hatred of the black other, is certainly encouraged in a society not yet purged of white supremacy.

On the searing track "Murder to Excellence," which appears on 2011's *Watch the Throne*, JAY-Z's album-length collaboration with Kanye West, the pair lament black-on-black crime. Jay, on the first part of the song, pleads for mutual respect among black men. He also calls out police killings of unarmed black folk and dedicates the verse to one such victim. Yet he assails the destructive impulse of black men to kill each other.

> *This is to the memory of Danroy Henry*
> *Too much enemy fire to catch a friendly*
> *Strays from the same shade nigga, we on the same*
>   *team*
> *Giving you respect, I expect the same thing*
> *All-black everything, nigga you know my fresh code*
> *I'm out here fighting for you, don't increase my stress*
>   *load*

The second part of the song offers an unusual antidote to black death—black wealth and the access that Jay and

Kanye's fame and fortune afford them. The song presents a provocative juxtaposition: decrying the violence that plagues mostly poor black communities and celebrating black exceptionalism as a tool of racial self-defense. Both Jay and Kanye rap about the exclusivity of black-tie affairs and what it means to sometimes be the only black guy in the room. Still, access to the upper echelons of American society, for Jay, Kanye, or anyone else, can hardly erase the social ills that dog the American experiment or substitute for social justice.

In Jay's third verse on "Murder to Excellence," he uses the game of dominoes as a metaphor for racial inequality. The player with the fewest number of black spots, or pips, on a domino tile wins with the higher score. The higher Jay rises, the fewer black folks he sees, and more white people come into play. Jay argues that it will take more than the success of token black elites like Will Smith and Oprah Winfrey to bring equality to the black masses:

Now please, domino, domino
Only spot a few blacks the higher up I go, uh
What's up Will? Uh, shout out to O, uh
That ain't enough, we gonna need a million more, uh

Nipsey's murder is for many a cautionary tale against staying in the hood to help instead of seeking refuge in the suburbs. Nipsey's life suggests the opposite is true: We need to flood working-class and poor communities with even more opportunities and majestic examples of neighborhood redemption.

JAY-Z's freestyle about Nipsey at Webster Hall featured as a prelude to his affecting "Some How Some Way," a song that confesses the desire to "make it up out the hood some day." On first blush it seems that Jay and Nipsey are at odds. But Jay ends his freestyle with a revealing couplet:

> *And we ain't gotta leave the hood physically*
> *But we gotta leave that shit mentally.*

Jay is invested in an ontology of ghetto existence that makes moral distinctions between helpful and destructive behavior. Not everything that happens in the ghetto should happen there. Contrary to the cliched credo, not all is good in the hood. It is not the physical geography that you have to escape but the destructive psychological habits and the existential threats that too often plague citizens of the hood.

Jay had earlier in his career reflected on the contrast between a hardcore hood mentality and the intelligence and maturity of a "real" hustler who does big things in the bigger world. His 2009 song "D.O.A. (Death of Auto-Tune)," proclaims,

> *I don't be in the project hallway*
> *Talking 'bout how I be in the project all day (uhh!)*
> *That sound stupid to me.*

He reinforces the point on 2009's "What We Talkin' About," when he highlights the difference between faking violent acts on digital platforms and leaving the hardcore habits behind for a taste of political royalty.

> *Now you could choose to sit in front of your computer*
> *Posin' with guns, shootin' YouTube up*
> *Or you could come with me to the White House, get*
>   *your suit up!*
> *You stuck on being hardcore, I chuck the deuce up.*

But it was JAY-Z's reflections on the philosophical underpinnings of Nipsey's community activism on his Webster Hall freestyle that drew the strongest reaction. JAY-Z explained Nipsey's efforts to revitalize and stabilize his neighborhood amid the foul winds of redlining, depressed assets, property seizures, a crabs-in-the-barrel mentality, the hardships of being hurt by some of the folk you aim to help, and the personal and financial distractions that hamper the pursuit of lasting goals and higher priorities. Jay did all of this in tight scope through a procession of carefully articulated a cappella bars. But controversy erupted over the first line he uttered in the effort to explain how structural forces like neighborhood design could foster a toxic environment for black urban dwellers.

> *Gentrify your own hood, before these people do it*
> *Claim eminent domain and have your people move in*

That's a small glimpse into what Nipsey was doing
For anybody that's still confused as to what he was
doing.

Critics on social media weighed in. They suggested that gentrification is the process of well-heeled, middle-class citizens or rich elites descending on a poor urban community and buying up and rehabbing its battered housing stock, causing a rise in property values and thus pushing out citizens because of financial hardship. Nipsey Hussle, they argued, was doing anything but that. Critics contended that JAY-Z was undermining Nipsey's legacy by promoting renovation that comes at the expense of residents who are least able to afford homes in communities that are vastly overhauled. By taking JAY-Z literally, his critics overlooked his aim to broaden the scope of Nipsey's work by highlighting his efforts to reconstitute the neighborhood through bright hustling and black entrepreneurship. Plus, Jay's critics spoke as if eminent domain is a governmental prerogative that individuals have no control over. And they contended that black folk couldn't, en masse, "buy back the block," as Jay and others suggested, because they couldn't get the loans and credit.

Gentrification has undoubtedly had disastrous effects. Neighborhoods have been waylaid by heartless developers itching to empty them of the pesky poor to make room for upwardly mobile professionals. The character of communities has often been dramatically altered too. Communal rituals, neighborhood practices, informal arrangements, occasions of celebration, and local benchmarks of progress have been wiped away under the punishing directives of crassly calculated—and grossly mislabeled—community development. And resources for upgrading or refinancing housing have been dramatically shifted from those in need to those in pursuit of more space for elevated homeownership, higher-quality goods, and expanded services denied to long-term residents.

Neither JAY-Z nor Nipsey ignored the devastating effects of gentrification. They both envisioned a healthy if complicated route to community development and neighborhood empowerment. When Jay urged black folk to take control of their hoods before others did so, he wasn't unaware of the difficult path to such a goal, including lack of capital investment and stunted borrowing. But he, like Nipsey, refused to see obstacles as permanent or failed opportunities as final. Their motto seemed to be: To the hustler go the spoils. These men were indeed hustlers who had often made a way where none had previously existed. They worked, in their earlier lives, in informal, underground economies against the powers that be. What more might they achieve if they could leverage the legitimacy they now possess in cooperation with government agencies and political figures? Sure, their fame gives access and breaks that ordinary folk can't get. But that didn't mean that Jay and Nipsey couldn't have led the way in opening opportunities in which others might participate. (And while eminent domain grants government the power to snatch private property for public use, that right can also be granted to corporations and individuals, a point that makes Jay's claim far less ridiculous than many asserted.)

Nipsey and his business partner, real estate investor David Gross, sought to use the political system to do just what Jay encouraged his listeners at Webster Hall to do. Nipsey also realized that he could generate projects that would facilitate investment by folk in the hood, granting them an ownership stake in their community economic development. Thus, Jay was right—they would gentrify their own hood before outside investors did. Sure, one could quibble with his wording, but it is clear that Jay and Nipsey were on the same page, had talked to each other about Nipsey's plans, and understood the need to hustle to make opportunity rain down. Through Nipsey and Gross's Our Opportunity investment fund, ordinary folk could enjoy economic development and invest in their own neighborhoods, not only in Los Angeles but, as the duo planned, in struggling communities across America.

That's why Nipsey was so beloved. At the time he died, not many people beyond his neighborhood knew about his forward-minded approach to community development. Nor did they realize just how big his heart and vision were. To his hood, he was them, and he realized that he became more of himself with their help.

In giving back, he responded to their desire to be more like him and, therefore, helped them to become more of themselves.

It seems that each day since Nipsey's death more of his words surface and shed light on the secular scriptures he spat in rhyme. His death at thirty-three inevitably suggests the trope of resurrection, or at least a biblical reckoning with his time on earth. It may seem farfetched to ruminate on the rumbling of the divine amid the violence Nipsey confronted. If Jesus is too great a comparison, then perhaps Hussle's notion of running a marathon is more in league with Apostle Paul. "I have fought the good fight, I have finished the race, I have kept the faith," he said. Or as Hussle said, "Hopin' as you walk across the sand you see my shoe print / And you follow 'til it change your life, it's all an evolution."

Nipsey's beliefs will continue to resonate because followers will keep his words alive. They will recite his lyrics, engage his ideas, and show love to the people he loved, especially poor and working-class black and brown folk. Jay's words will continue to echo because his words help keep us alive to truth. Their meaning couldn't be more relevant than it is now in a cultural fight on many fronts. We now confront resurgent bigotry, increased antiblack sentiment, and the weaponizing of "otherness" to scare the white masses. Poor black folk need strong voices like JAY-Z's in the culture to plead their case and defend their humanity.

One of the greatest virtues of JAY-Z's hustling is certainly how it inspires icons like LeBron and Nipsey. But it inspires millions of ordinary folks too. And it translates black ideas about society in a compelling fashion. Black hustle has transformed American life, from the underground to the playground, from tough streets to corporate suites, from the crack house to the White House. JAY-Z has created greater appreciation for black hustle by helping to launch hip hop into the cultural stratosphere. Once deemed a genre that was musically inferior and without artistic merit, hip hop has become the culture's lingua franca and the globe's measure of both cool and rebellion.

It is noteworthy that a former crack dealer has transformed the image of black hustle by using the wiles of the underground to conquer American business. It is more remarkable that his historic rise is rooted in rhetoric, in words to explain black hustle and, therefore, black genius to the world. He has also adhered to a central tenet of hip hop: don't defer to whiteness and don't genuflect before the altar of American grammar. Instead, he invited America to bow at the shrine of hip hop's language and to understand the genius of the black youth the country feared, ignored, detested, relegated to the projects, or forced into the underground.

I made it so you could say Marcy and it was all good
I ain't crossover I brought the suburbs to the hood

*Made 'em relate to your struggle, told 'em 'bout
     your hustle*
Went on MTV with do-rags, I made them love you
*You know normally them people wouldn't be fuckin'
     witchu*
'Til I made 'em understand why you do what you do

Those lines from 1999's "Come and Get Me" neatly sum up one of the great rationales of rap: to make "them people"—the people who control commerce and construct prisons, who assign seats in schools and give out jobs, who greenlight films and redline neighborhoods, who write scathing reports about black life, who pack poor blacks into ghettoes and leave healthy food out of the local grocery store, who largely loan money to folk who look like them, who give the benefit of the doubt to others in their own neighborhoods, who shoot black folk out of hate or fear—understand young black folk, particularly the poor and hurting.

JAY-Z is the only rap superstar over 40 and there is no roadmap for how to sustain popularity, to fulfill expectations for what is the unarticulated norm. Thus, within his brilliance there has to be an idea or strategy for how to . . . transition . . . from lyrics of the 26 year old leaving drug dealing behind to telling stories of women in a way that lifts them up.

TONI BLACKMAN

By not acknowledging the deep visceral pleasures black youth derive from making and consuming culture . . . these authors reduce expressive culture to a political text . . . But what counts more than the story is the "storytelling"—an emcee's verbal facility on the mic, the creative and often hilarious use of puns, metaphors, similes, not to mention the ability to kick some serious slang (or what we might call linguistic inventiveness).

ROBIN D. G. KELLEY

"I Paint Pictures with Poems"

POETRY

As strange as it may sound, JAY-Z is an underrated rapper. Yes, he is recognized for his swaggering self-confidence and astonishing verbal gifts. But he is not nearly as celebrated for his vivid and extremely sophisticated romp on poetry's playground of metaphor and metonymy, simile and synecdoche. He is Robert Frost with a Brooklyn accent, Rita Dove with a Jesus piece.

Jay is a past master of American poesy. He composes in the recording studio with the tools of verse at hand. He is an architect of sound whose rhymes satisfy the ear. He is a painter of images whose visions flood the mind's eye. He sketches verbal blueprints that map the black experience onto American rhetoric. As he makes his way to the recording booth, Jay stumbles over discarded stanzas, fumbles with multiple forms, trips on loitering tropes.

He chisels away at the air until sound becomes sense and words are sculpted from mumbles. Meanwhile, Jay is ambushed by double entendres, and instead of turning them over to English authorities, he plays judge and jury and gives them long sentences.

Jay's lyrical cleverness masks his deeper intellectual reflections on the world and on black culture itself. Jay's claim in "Moment of Clarity," that "I dumbed down for my audience to double my dollars," is a misdirection of sorts. "Moment of Clarity" is one of the clearest explanations of the logic behind his approach to making commercial music with intellectual heft. Jay asks his listeners to study intently his body of work—from *Reasonable Doubt* to the *Black Album,* on which the song appears. He promises them that if they'll "[l]isten close, you'll hear what I'm about."

Jay realizes that the knock on him is that he treads water at the shallow end of the pool. In order to get his audience to at least hear what he has to say, and to discover how well he can handle the deep end, he has to first get them into the water—that is, sell records. By first advertising himself as an accessible pop culture figure, and not a daunting thinker, Jay can invite his listeners into the waters of reflection as an intellectual lifeguard of sorts with the promise that they won't get in over their heads. This is the same man, after all, who had established his trustworthiness as a well-informed guide who wouldn't burden his listeners with obscure language and esoteric ideas. In a battle with a foe who didn't have to be named, Jay makes it plain that his opponent, known for being an intellectual heavyweight, was outwardly impressive but lacked true substance.

> *And y'all buy the shit, caught up in the hype*
> *'Cause the nigga wear a kufi, don't mean that he*
>   *bright*
> *'Cause you don't understand him, it don't mean*
>   *that he nice*
> *It just means you don't understand all the bullshit*
>   *that he write*

Jay argues on "Moment of Clarity" that if he took the tack of gifted rappers of conscience like Talib Kweli and Common he wouldn't be commercially viable. Despite his admiration for them, their enormous skills haven't created a big pay day or wide cultural influence. This isn't the fault of the artists but a reflection of how the culture operates. Jay says that rappers must make up their minds about what their goals are and how they intend to achieve them. He makes clear that his goal is to help the poor—and his hustling history tells him that making music that sells is one way to do that. But he claims that underneath it all is a cunning intelligence that fosters strategies of wealth creation and resource sharing.

> *Fuck perception! Go with what makes sense*
> *Since I know what I'm up against*
> *We as rappers must decide what's most important*

And I can't help the poor if I'm one of them
So I got rich and gave back, to me that's the win/win
So next time you see the homie and his rims spin
Just know my mind is working just like them (rims,
     that is)

Jay's edifying and strategic misdirection didn't keep
the depth of his gift from sounding through. His first
album, *Reasonable Doubt*, teems with complex metaphors
like these lines from "Can I Live":

My mind is infested with sick thoughts that circle
Like a Lexus, if driven wrong it's sure to hurt you
Dual level like duplexes, in unity
My crew and me commit atrocities like we got
     immunity

And his rhymes revel in intricate wordplay, like this
from "D'Evils":

She said the taste of dollars was shitty, so I fed her
     fifties
About his whereabouts I wasn't convinced
I kept feedin' her money 'til her shit started to make
     sense.

The eye more easily captures the meaning on a page,
or onscreen, in hindsight, after careful reading, but the

ear must hear the lyrics repeatedly to get their full meaning. Such is the nature of JAY-Z's craft. The claim to dumb things down is meant to allay the fear of depth. Jay loses none of his sophistication in his strategy to say smart things in an accessible fashion. He layers his lyrics with multiple meanings; he waxes philosophical and poetic while keeping the party lights on.

When *Reasonable Doubt* debuted in 1996, it wasn't instantly hailed as a classic by critics. That designation had to wait a couple of years. In 1998, *Source* magazine, the hip hop Bible at the time, revised its initial rating of four out of five mics and gave the album a perfect five mics. Neither was the album eagerly snapped up by consumers. *Reasonable Doubt* wouldn't garner platinum-level sales until 2002, by which time JAY-Z had become a big star. From that point forward, he left nothing to chance.

Jay learned the lesson not to wear his learning so heavily. His strategy to obscure his erudition as he spoke his piece had many aspects. It was a matter of modifying his themes. Jay made a calculated effort to disguise his intelligence by scattering his philosophical reflections on life amid lyrical nods to the good life in clubs or cars. It was also a matter of proportion. For every "Minority Report," reflecting on Hurricane Katrina, or "Young, Gifted & Black," a colorful indictment of white privilege, there were many more of "I Just Wanna Love U (Give it 2 Me)," a gleeful ode to bacchanalia and booty.

His approach was also a matter of placement and

priority. Jay has made quite a few "B-sides," songs not released as singles or deemed to be hits. These efforts afforded Jay greater freedom to explore his wide-ranging interests without fear that his complex wordplay or rich literacy might scare listeners away. Many of these songs contain the "eggs" he places on each album for aficionados to hunt for, for true lovers of Jay's sophisticated poetry to seek out. A vibrant example is 1997's "Streets Is Watching," where Jay reflects on his divine destiny as he negotiates the treacherous code of the streets:

> *Was this a lesson God teaching me? Was he saying that*
> *I was playing the game straight from Hell from*
> *   which few came back?*
> *Like bad coke, pimp or die, was my mind frame back*
> *When niggas was thinking simplify, was turning*
> *   cocaine crack*
> *Ain't a whole lot of brain to that, just trying to*
> *   maintain a stack*

On 2002's "Don't You Know," Jay celebrates his embodiment of the poetic vocation by personifying his craft.

> *Won't you throw in the towel? I'm better with*
> *   vowels*
> *My vocabulary murders the dictionary*
> *Flow switches every 16, shit mean, man*
> *. . .*

Nigga I'm poetry
In four-part harmony, it's like Jodeci
Check out my melody, my flow is a felony.

Jay returned on later songs to the tension between art and commerce. He said, point blank on "The Prelude," in 2006, that "Bein' intricate'll get you wood, critic." Wood, as in a disc not going platinum, or gold, but selling very few records. On 1998's "Hard Knock Life (Ghetto Anthem)," Jay reminded his audience of its offense:

I gave you prophecy on my first joint, and y'all all
*   lamed out*
Didn't really appreciate it 'til the second one came out.

In 2007, on "Ignorant Shit," before he begins to rap, Jay complains about the lukewarm critical reception of his previous album, 2006's *Kingdom Come.*

Y'all niggas got me really confused out there
I make "Big Pimpin" or "Give it 2 Me," one of those
Y'all hail me as the greatest writer of the 21st century
I make some thought provokin' shit
Y'all question whether he fallin' off?

Jay's one-time rival Nas said it directly on "Let There Be Light": "I can't sound smart, 'cause y'all will run away."

Still, Jay's lyric from "Moment of Clarity" has social

and racial purpose: Jay can preserve the complex and coded conversations he has in his music, for instance, with folk who are still hustling or with those whose racial struggles tie them to him. And then, at his discretion, he can, as the title of his memoir suggests, decode his work, both for those who are new to his lyrics and for those who wonder just what he may have had in mind as they pore over his secular scriptures.

Perhaps we have not given him sufficient credit because our bias against hip hop artists won't let us see that the best of them have at the ready an army of narrative techniques to tell their stories and spread their truths. Jay has proved his mettle and pedigree as a poet through the sophisticated use of literary devices and refined craft. He has proved it by arguing persuasively that intelligence is a highly desirable good. He's shown it through the use of hyperbole and braggadocio, and by his ingenious extension of the black oral tradition. He's also given us a glimpse of his poetic gifts, and underscored his remarkable longevity, by engaging three of the greatest artists of his time.

He had beef in the late nineties and early aughts with legendary wordsmith and Queens MC Nas. He had brotherhood and camaraderie with fellow Brooklyn icon The Notorious B.I.G. (born Christopher Wallace) before Biggie's murder in 1997. And, on and off, over the last decade, he has had collaborations and competition with biracial Canadian rap superstar Drake. He and Drake have in particular clashed over how Jay uses poetry to spotlight visual art.

Jay not only enthusiastically embraces the visual and performance arts, but he grapples with his identity as a hustler, with racial strife and black identity, with black cultural habits and traits, and with the function of art, high and low, in the pursuit of meaningful existence. He has also used poetry to probe the relationship between rappers and superheroes.

If critics miss Jay's literary sophistication, his high intelligence, his cosmopolitan cultural habits, his adroit readings of social life, his adept deconstructions of pop culture, his public intellectual labor, perhaps it is because, as JAY-Z says, they insist on a shallow reading of his art. They end up doing, ironically enough, the very thing they accuse him of, namely, sticking to the surface. Jay summarizes the claim and counters it on 2001's "Renegade," produced by Eminem:

Motherfuckers say that I'm foolish, I only talk about jewels (Bling bling)
Do you fools listen to music, or do you just skim through it?
See, I'm influenced by the ghetto you ruined
The same dude you gave nothin', I made somethin' doin'

What I do, through and through and
I give you the news with a twist, it's just his ghetto
  point of view.

In the opening lines of "Streets Is Watching," JAY-Z's classic treatise on drug dealer paranoia and angst, he seizes on the question of intelligence in hustling, hip hop, and beyond, and sends it our way.

Look, if I shoot you, I'm brainless
But if you shoot me, then you're famous
What's a nigga to do?

Jay poses the rhetorical question like it's an existential crisis. For those hustling on the corner, it is surely a Rubicon that, once crossed, commits them to action. Rhetoric and performance are now tied in Jay's view; they are critical to answer the question of how one uses what one learns to set a new standard for wisdom and behavior. All of this is driven by a regard for how acute observation and tough-minded reflection can help one to navigate the perils of the underground economy and to flourish while there—that is, as long as one can stay alive while plotting one's elevation or escape. There is the possibility that the narrator might act, or shoot, without proper forethought, without counting the cost. Thus, there is reckoning with the mortal effects of the drug dealing enterprise in toto.

There is, too, grappling with the consequences of specific actions. In particular, there is the potential for brainless decisions that can turn fatal within the cutthroat capitalism of the underground drug world.

Even after many listens, one thing is clear: the opening lyrics and the song itself are smarter than they sound. The narrator urges listeners to "Smarten up, the streets is watching." His audience includes all sorts of hustlers, and himself as well, a dealer-turned-artist who has had to make smart decisions in his transition out of the drug economy. The song presents a pitch-perfect personification of the "streets" as an urban proxy of the surveillance state. Jay's narrator also makes multiple references to his state of mind to paint a bleak picture of the world that many critics accuse JAY-Z of mindlessly glamorizing. The lyrics come down on the side of drug dealing, finally, as a non-thinking enterprise. "Ain't a whole lot of brain to that," he says, concluding that the decision to leave behind the violent, communally debilitating life of the drug dealer is an easy one. "[W]hy risk myself, I just write it in rhymes." Or more to the point: "This unstable way of living just had to stop."

"Kingdom Come," the title track from JAY-Z's 2006 comeback album—he briefly retired in 2003 to become CEO of Def Jam after releasing *The Black Album*—offers a paradigm of intelligence as a desirable good that greatly serves an audience composed of hustlers.

And I'm so evolved I'm so involved
I'm showing growth, I'm so in charge
. . .
I'm so indebted, I should have been deaded
Selling blow in the park, this I know in my heart
Now I'm so enlightened I might glow in the dark.

Traditional notions of public intellectual work usually root knowledge in the ivory towers of the university. The spread of knowledge is then traced into the busy lives of everyday folk who normally can't get to the learning the academy so viciously polices. In a way, JAY-Z has reversed this trajectory. His artistic work has done what some of our most important academic work only aspires to achieve. He speaks to those in the underground economies, and they hear him. In fact, after his retirement, he heard the chorus of pleas for him to return to form.

I hear "hurry up Hov" when I'm out in the public
Cause niggas like: "but you love it; you be it, you're
   of it
"You breathe it, we need it; bring it back to the
   hustlas."

Princeton professor Imani Perry, in the *Chronicle of Higher Education*, has reflected on what the term "public" has to do with the phrase "public intellectual." For Perry, thinkers like writer and former NAACP head James Weldon Johnson and author and sociologist Anna Julia Cooper set the mark for what we should expect from public thinkers who ideally "desire to contribute in diverse ways." Perry says that there "is so much work to be done, particularly in communities of color, on a wide range of issues, including educational outcomes, imprisonment, nutrition, political representation, unemployment." The work of public thinkers can certainly help solve many of these problems.

JAY-Z has checked marks in many of these categories: he established the Shawn Carter Scholarship for the formerly incarcerated and for disadvantaged youth who want to go to college; helped to form an organization to promote criminal justice reform; became a vocal advocate for bail reform; produced documentaries that address the tragic deaths of Kalief Browder and Trayvon Martin; visibly supported Barack Obama and Hillary Clinton at different times in their runs for the Oval Office; and used his social media platforms and other outlets to promote a healthy lifestyle to his followers, which he backed up with an investment of a million dollars in a black-owned vegan cookie company. There are, too, his *New York Times* opinion pieces on social and criminal justice issues, his financial contributions to 9/11 victims and Hurricane Katrina survivors, his aid to black folk in need of legal support for police brutality and free speech cases, his paying the taxes of rap superstars Lil Wayne and Meek Mill and putting up money to bail out members of the Movement for Black Lives. I will explore at length in the next chapter his ideas about social change, racial injustice, and politics. But it is clear, both on record and beyond the sound booth, that Jay has solidified his status as a thinker and artist. His ideas about the underground, education, politics, and society have been translated into practical action and have influenced millions to think about important issues.

In "Hola Hovito," on his outstanding 2001 album *The Blueprint*, JAY-Z boldly claims that he "rhyme[s] sicker than every rhyme-spitter." Literary critics would argue that that's a clear case of hyperbole, a rhetorical means to accent the truth of his artistic superiority. Poetic principle in service of professional self-promotion. What can't be argued is that JAY-Z's lyrics exult in the lively and luxurious use of such poetic devices. It may be his promiscuous rendezvous with the figurative that makes him the "sickest" rhyme spitter of all time. But hyperbole is only the top layer of this particular lyric. The reconfiguration of "sick" as a metaphorical superlative has important roots in the culture. Rap music and African American Vernacular English (AAVE) are frequently spiced with ample doses of contronym, a literary mark of playful duality where a two-faced term can suggest its polar opposite in the right context.

Consider Run-DMC's great line, "Not bad meaning bad, but bad meaning good." Within the lexical universe of hip hop, "sick" borrows its most useful double from one of the culture's classic contronyms: "ill." Contronymic terms in hip hop tend toward the superlative spectrum of meaning.

The relentless quest for language that adequately describes what black folk experience fuels the refiguring of the negative as the positive. Hence there is a moral meaning attached to the use of language in black life. Making it plain that speech has ethical consequences helps to filter a certain set of experiences through the prism of hip hop lyrics. A useful analogy can be made between rapping and preaching. Rappers can be conceived as evangelists who promote the idea that something can come from nothing and that negative circumstances might produce positive outcomes. Theology and sociology nicely combine. Life in the hood can be ill—that is, sick—undoubtedly in a negative way, but sick, too, in the superlative sense conjured in the contronymic figuration of the word. JAY-Z makes a compelling claim to be the sickest ever "rhyme-spitter," even though every generation sends formidable rappers to the microphone. And even though most rhymes are more spoken than spit. But that might lead us down a literary rabbit hole where we debate whether metaphor or metonym best suits the case.

"Guns & Roses," the song, not the iconic rock group of the same name, is one of JAY-Z's most intriguing collaborations. "Guns & Roses" was produced in 2002 by the late, great rapper Heavy D. There are vocal and guitar contributions from Lenny Kravitz, whose rock-tinged licks underscore lyrics that wrestle with the violence and bliss that shape the ups and downs of hustling and rap music. As usual Jay proclaims his artistic greatness.

> *The Michael Corleone of the microphone*
> *The Michelangelo of flow, I paint pictures with poems.*

Allusions matter, like those to Italian icons of American pop culture and the High Renaissance, and I'll get to them soon. But the punch line, "I paint pictures with poems," is as important an analogy as Jay has ever articulated. In one line, he evokes his career-long allusions to Warhol, Picasso, and Michelangelo, his direct engagement with museum culture, and his affinity and affection for Jean-Michel Basquiat. JAY-Z does not write his rhymes in a traditional sense—and yes, more on that later, too—so it may be more accurate to argue that he crafts his images through words. This is more than poetic imagery; it harkens back to the early-twentieth-century poetic movement known as Imagism. That movement featured giants like Ezra Pound and James Joyce and a call for precise, concrete images drawn from common speech, rhythmic inventiveness, and unlimited topics of engagement, all meant to forge clear expression. It can be argued that the best rap artists embrace the Poundian and Joycean imperatives, but none more, or better, than JAY-Z.

Jay's sublime attraction to poetic and literary devices has been fed by thousands of hours of exercising his craft. That befits his admiration for Malcolm Gladwell, who popularized the notion that mastery is achieved with at least ten thousand hours of practice. Although he told Oprah in *O* magazine in 2009 that English was his favorite subject in high school, and that Homer's *The Odyssey* left him feeling dreamy about life partnerships and the concept of returning home, Jay has had little formal training in the craft of writing poetry. His practice, still, has almost always been intentional, a reference to another of his favorite books that explores the spiritual dimensions of intentional living, Gary Zukav's *The Seat of the Soul*. That practice began on the street corners of Brooklyn, New York. In a hidden track on *The Blueprint* album, JAY-Z extends the analogy of lyrically working out on "Breathe Easy (Lyrical Exercise)." The track opens *in medias res* with an interview snippet where Jay describes his writing process. While standing on the corner, dealing crack, Jay would craft and rehearse his rhymes in his mind until he had both perfected and memorized them. "Breathe Easy" bobs and weaves seamlessly through at least three forms of exercise, including jogging, sparring, and weightlifting. There are verses but no real hook except for the extended analogy itself. Jay is rapping about the exercise of rapping using the language of exercise itself. As he brags on the track, he's in great shape.

Braggadocio is the pervasive ethos of JAY-Z's music.

If the repetition of a statement or a concept makes it a perceived reality, then Jay has consistently reminded us of how real his greatness is. Given the accumulation of lyrical repetition at work in JAY-Z's boasting about his gifts, the simplest lines at times deliver the most powerful figurative effects. Take his line "flyer than a piece of paper bearin' my name" from "Public Service Announcement." Paper fliers are paper advertisements that are widely distributed by mail, posted in public places, or passed on to individuals. They have an important place in the history of hip hop. In fact, hip hop fliers are enshrined in the Harvard Hiphop Archive and Research Institute, the Cornell University Hip Hop Collection, and the National Museum of African American History and Culture. They are concrete, well, metaphorically at least, and if not concrete, then material representations of the culture.

The concept of the flier in hip hop flies effortlessly in and through this one line. The flier is an example of an image carefully stamped in a lyric that represents JAY-Z's artistic signature. A throwaway line becomes a classic, much the same way that a flier to be thrown away becomes a hip hop staple. (Of course most fliers were single-page advertisements without need of a staple, except to pin them to a tree or billboard, just as Jay's line helped to pin down the performance of "Public Service Announcement.")

But there is more. Flight in African American culture has deep conceptual resonance. There are historical aspirations to flee bondage and to imagine being able to fly away from captivity. The modern notion of being or looking "fly" is all about style and sartorial excellence. Of course, when Jay suggests that he is flyer than a flier, a nifty homophone where the words sound the same but have different meanings, he breaks and enters into their homophonic connection to gain figurative access to the wealth of their suggestive meanings. (He also plays on the multiple meanings of the term on 2006's "Beach Chair," where he says, "Son said: 'Hov', how you get so fly?' / I said: 'From not being afraid to fall out the sky.'") It is at least a triple entendre embedded in braggadocio that is committed to the poetic principles of Imagism while paying homage to a key artifact of hip hop's material culture.

As a writer, I find it astonishing that JAY-Z does not write down his lyrics. He does not impress paper with ink in order to impress his hearers with his complex rhymes. He does not so much as scribble his thoughts on paper or type them on any surface or screen. Given the huge quantity and high quality of his oeuvre, his work is all the more remarkable. Orality is a defining feature of black culture. The oral tradition of crafting and transmitting African American folktales was inherited by enslaved Africans from their continental forebearers. These oral stories were designed to make sense of the brutal conditions foisted on black souls in the New World during the long siege of transatlantic slavery. Folktales from the African oral tradition seeped into the fabric of black expression and performance. One popular example, "The People Who Could Fly," captures the incredible story of mass suicide by Africans in bondage. The story is transformed into a celebration of resistance and liberation in the face of racial violence and chattel slavery. There is little doubt that hip hop culture creatively extends the moral instincts of the oral tradition. As a hip hop writer, JAY-Z epitomizes black orality in the twenty-first century.

But Jay doesn't primarily rap about slavery. His most profound contributions to the African American oral tradition are more like hustler turned author Iceberg Slim than novelist Charles Chesnutt. ("Where's Iceberg Slim he was the coldest cat?" say those asking JAY-Z to come out of retirement on "Kingdom Come.") Instead Jay has made high art of low culture. Some of his most salient contributions to the African American oral tradition are gritty and at times violent narratives that portray underground economies in the waning years of the twentieth century. "Friend or Foe," from 1996's *Reasonable Doubt*, and 1998's "Friend or Foe '98," from *In My Lifetime, Volume 1*, are two classic examples of this form.

Neither of these are best described as songs. "Friend or Foe" has a run time of about 1:50 and "Friend or Foe '98" clocks in at just over two minutes. Neither track has any semblance of a hook. Both performances in tandem complete the story of how Jay's narrator first warns and then disposes of his would-be competition in the drug game. The style of the lyrics is conversational and flippant, downplaying the sort of cutthroat approaches to the turf wars that plague illegal drug dealing. The setting is "out-of-state," and in "Friend or Foe," with piercing staccato horns blowing away, Jay's narrator advises his opponent to never "ever-ever-ever-ever-ever-ever come around here no mo'."

In "Friend or Foe '98," fretful guitars dominate the soundscape as his competition returns with schemes to murder Jay's narrator. His opponent is foiled, and Jay's narrator kills him, and in the process of pulling the trigger, sends salutations and "ice cubes" to his recently departed friend, Biggie Smalls. The "Friend or Foe" tag team was not designed for radio airplay. The songs don't have, nor do they require, music videos. Each is its own cinematic glimpse into the life of a New York drug dealer hustling in Virginia, or elsewhere in the South, only to find that some other Northeastern hustler has the same idea of making easy money where the demand is high, law enforcement is soft, and competition is limited.

Jay's vocal performance, particularly on the original "Friend or Foe," sounds effortless. The recording plays more like a freestyle than a premeditated "written" set of rhymes. This is both intentional and a consequence of Jay's artistic process. The lyrical work sounds unrehearsed and therefore more authentic and, in this sense, more easily absorbed into an established African American oral tradition. But the unrehearsed free-flowing aesthetic of the

"Friend or Foe" verses also reflects JAY-Z's non-writing "writing" process. That process in turn helps to bolster the aesthetic and epic nature of the "Friend or Foe" conflict. The aesthetic requires a demeanor in the narrator that is effortlessly cool but ultimately calculating given the stakes of this illegal "game." Revisiting the "Friend or Foe" narratives reminds listeners of the prelude to JAY-Z's "Breathe Easy (Lyrical Exercise)," where he talks specifically about committing lyrics to memory as he navigates urban corners, hustling his illegal product.

JAY-Z's lyrical process itself feels a tad illegal, as if his gifts violate some unwritten law, as if not writing words down and using mnemonic tricks should not lead to artistic dominance. JAY-Z's artistic process forces us to rethink exactly what it means to write, which should be reimagined, at least in his case, as an operation exclusively using the mind.

We often consider metaphor to be the figurative tool of choice for MCs and rappers. That is a subtle allusion to the fact that aficionados make a distinction between kinds of rhetorical creativity. MCs master the mic with technical skills and verbal dexterity. Rappers command the mic with political passion or personal zeal. But the art of allusion has quietly become a major component of all great hip hop songs. Allusions thrive as implied references and have always been near the top of Jay's creative chamber. Much of Jay's artistic swagger relies on the implications of his proven ability to survive the pitfalls of hustling in America. Thus his body of work regularly alludes to his life as a hustler. This "macro" allusion to his life experiences requires him to tap into the underground world of drug dealing in the belief that his audience shares some measure of the experience with him. And yet from the time of his first release, 1996's *Reasonable Doubt*, most of Jay's audience wasn't standing on urban corners "slinging" crack rocks. But something artistically transformative occurred. Jay's allusions to hustling assumed an audience that understood the experiences he detailed in his lyrics. There was an allusive connection between an ex-hustler rapping about hustling and his audience of hustlers. That allusive connection in turn provided all of Jay's listeners an authentic sense of the experiences he alluded to in order to create the music in the first place.

Allusions often require a lyrical leap of faith that the person, figure, text, art, or piece of literature the poet suggests can be easily discerned by her audience. That discernment is driven by the shared experiences that underwrite the figurative force of allusions. After Biggie's untimely death, Jay repeatedly cited his fallen friend on record. Each citation of Biggie is a self-contained allusion to him. These allusions—and Jay's recurring citation of Biggie's lyrics or references to them in various ways—form an ongoing tribute to his comrade and permit Jay's audience to share the experience with him. In this case it is the experience of loss and the mourning that attends the brutal public murder of an iconic hip hop figure.

These and other poetic concerns are at play in JAY-Z's richly allusive "Meet the Parents," from his 2002 *The Blueprint 2* album. In his memoir *Decoded*, Jay writes that he "never intended 'Meet the Parents' to be subtle," and yet the subtleties of this track abound. "Meet the Parents" has a powerful effect for first-time listeners that will be ruined by my exposition. The title "Meet the Parents" alludes to the great Ben Stiller movies of the same name. (As a sixty-year-old black man, I harken back as well to the film *Guess Who's Coming to Dinner*, in which a black physician, played by acting idol Sidney Poitier, meets for the first time his white fiancée's liberal parents, played by screen legends Spencer Tracy and Katharine Hepburn, who have no idea in advance of his race.) Stiller's 2000 film *Meet the Parents,* directed by Jay Roach, and also starring Robert De Niro and Blythe Danner, was a remake of a 1992 film of the same name directed by Greg Glienna. Stiller's *Meet the Parents* was popular enough to inspire two sequels, *Meet the Fockers* and *Little Fockers*, and two television shows, the situation comedy *In-Laws* and the reality-television show *Meet My Folks*, both of which debuted in 2002. There's no doubt that Stiller's *Meet the Parents* was an apt allusion that easily worked in the collective consciousness of JAY-Z's listeners. The film humorously details a time-honored tradition of life partners meeting each other's families. Stiller's version of this tradition stews in the anxiety that these situations often provoke. It is pure comedy. Jay's "Meet the Parents" is decidedly darker, an epic tragedy.

JAY-Z's "Meet the Parents" exposes without effort the unspoken white and class privileges that fuel *Meet the Parents*. In the film, two upper-middle-class families come together before the upcoming nuptials of Greg Focker (played by Ben Stiller) and Pam Byrnes (played by Teri Polo). The film highlights the cultural differences between the Byrneses, a white Anglo-Saxon Protestant family, and the Fockers, a white American Jewish family. "Meet the Parents" is about a monumental inner-city one-night stand between two characters named Isis and Mike. Their brief union produced the unnamed protagonist of JAY-Z's tale. Isis loves Mike for all the wrong reasons.

> *Mike was the hard head from around the way*
> *That she wanted all her life, shit, she wanted all the*
> *hype.*

Mike immediately denies his paternity and absolves himself of any fatherly responsibility. "If that was my son, he would look much different," he says. Mike disconnects from his son and from Isis. The decision by the father to not claim or care for his son is one with which JAY-Z personally identifies, since his father left home when Jay was eleven years old. It was a tragic and defining moment for the young Shawn Carter. As an internationally renowned artist, Jay takes a moment to allude to his pain and to underscore the pain of black fathers who abandon their kids.

But "Meet the Parents" functions lyrically as a composite of interlocking allusions. More tragedy looms for Isis, Mike, and their unnamed son. Fourteen years go by in "Meet the Parents" without Mike and Isis speaking and without Mike talking to his son. In a Shakespearean twist of events, Mike confronts a young hustler on the urban strip where he normally hustles. He tells the younger man to move along, and the younger man bristles. They face off and draw weapons on each other, each armed with a snub-nose thirty-eight pistol. The younger man hesitates because he sees a glimmer of himself in the older man's face. That bit of hesitation proves to be deadly as the older man fires six shots, killing the younger man. Jay's narrator provides the costly moral lesson as the song concludes.

> *Six shots into his kin out of the gun*
> *Niggas, be a father, you killin' your sons*

Jay repeats the lines for emphasis and chilling effect.

Black fatherlessness has often been prompted by draconian public policies like unjust prison sentencing and counterproductive housing rules. It has also been overblown by media coverage and made political fodder for right-wing and liberal interests. But the allusion to *Meet the Parents* is a powerful reminder that the challenges of parenting and absenteeism in African American communities are real. "Meet the Parents" may not be so subtle in its jarring contrast of black fatherlessness and the easy paternal privilege of the film it alludes to. But the figure of Isis demands a deeper reading as we grapple with black rituals of mourning. After seeing her son's dead body in the morgue, Isis's

> *addiction grew, prescription drugs, sippin' brew*
> *Angel dust, dipped in WOO!*

She is as tragic a figure as either of the men who draw on each other in the song. In too many painful ways, Isis embodies the modern black mother in mourning. We know these mothers, Sybrina Fulton, Leslie McSpadden, and Lucy McBath among them. They are women who are forced into a sorority of suffering to publicly mourn children lost to senseless violence by the police or by black folk. It is telling that Isis is the name of the Egyptian goddess of mourning. When her husband Osiris is killed by her brother Seth, her mourning becomes mythic and divine. With her divine magical prowess, she reassembles her husband's body and brings him briefly back to life. But ultimately Osiris cannot remain among the living and becomes the king of the dead. This establishes Isis as the goddess of mourning and the queen of the dead. The myth of Isis is a family affair in Egyptian lore, and JAY-Z taps into that timeless mythology, connecting it to the challenges that we face in contemporary urban and black communities. "Meet the Parents" is a mythic tribute of its own. It is a warning to its listeners of the perilous outcomes of forsaken parenting, and an indelible paean to those who struggle to survive the neighbor-to-neighbor, father-to-son, and brother-to-brother violence that plagues our communities.

It is ironic that Jay's conscientious rebuke to intramural black violence came in the recent aftermath of his epic row with Nas. By every measure the lyrical war on and off record between Shawn Carter and Nasir Jones was the best "beef" in hip hop history. Their government names are interchangeable with their rap monikers here—and only here—given the personal nature of aspects of their pugilistic exchange. By the time most of us started to pay attention to the Nas and Jay conflict, there was already a greater war unfolding. Shots had already been fired when JAY-Z took the stage at Summer Jam 2001 and teased the world with the first bars of "Takeover." Summer Jam is the annual hip hop summer festival sponsored since 1994 by New York–based radio station Hot 97. That year it took place in Long Island's Nassau Coliseum.

Many followers of the New York rhyme scene had been paying attention since Nas bragged that a Lexus with television sets in it was the "minimum" luxury car one should enjoy, a direct jab at JAY-Z's vehicle choice in 1996. Some say the beef predated this slight, to when Nas failed to show up for the "Dead Presidents II" studio session for JAY-Z's debut album, *Reasonable Doubt*. (To outsiders these jabs and offenses feel light; their heaviness is determined by how they signify in a syntax of insult and a grammar of grievance driven by turf, tone, and testosterone.) Ironically Nas's physical absence from the recording session turned into his sampled presence on the song. Producer Ski Beatz interpolated Nas's vocals from "The World Is Yours" into "Dead Presidents II." That song in turn became one of JAY-Z's signature recordings.

JAY-Z's opening salvo in this battle was a boast of membership in rap's pantheon. On 1997's "Where I'm From," he contends that hip hop partisans

argue all day about
Who's the best MCs—Biggie, Jay-Z, or Nas.

Jay was then a young upstart with only one record to his credit. Claiming comparable status to Nas and Biggie may have seemed premature. But these lines rang true. True enough, *Reasonable Doubt* only got its just due after

JAY-Z gained prominence, even if some fans spotted its lyrical pedigree from the start. But discussions about JAY-Z's capabilities as an MC were already drawing "G.O.A.T." (Greatest Of All Time) comparisons.

Jay began this beef in earnest at Summer Jam when he declared, "Ask Nas, he don't want it with Hov. NO!" That line got tongues wagging all over the hip hop universe. Consider the context. The first thirty bars or so of the "Takeover" are directed at Queens hip hop duo Mobb Deep, composed of rappers Havoc and Prodigy.

> *I don't care if you Mobb Deep, I hold triggers to crews*
> *You little fuck, I got money stacks bigger than you*
> *When I was pushin' weight back in '88*
> *You was a ballerina, I got the pictures, I seen ya*
> *Then you dropped "Shook Ones," switched your*
>   *demeanor*
> *Well, we don't believe you, you need more people.*

It was a spot-on verbal tirade that challenged the group's hood bona fides because of Jay's withering disbelief in their claims of toughness. It left the authors of "Shook Ones" a bit shaken themselves. Although Jay claimed, "I got the pictures, I seen ya," the actual photos that Jay flashed on the screen at Summer Jam showed Prodigy in a *Thriller*-era Michael Jackson outfit, with a multiple-zippered jacket, white socks, and black loafers. The photos were snapped by Prodigy's grandmother as he performed as a boy for her dance studio's annual recital at a New York concert hall. Interestingly, at the same Summer Jam concert where he dissed Prodigy and Nas, Jay brought out Michael Jackson in a spectacular cameo appearance, thus undercutting his diss of Prodigy and signifying that he actually embraced Jackson.

The diss of Prodigy was an instance of Jay playing the dozens, a game with long roots in black culture where insults are exchanged in a ritual verbal battle between contestants. Prodigy thought the display of the photos was funny and took no offense. He told me as much when we had a public conversation about his autobiography, *My Infamous Life*, six years before his death in 2017. He also said he had encountered Jay outside a New York restaurant a few months after the Summer Jam incident. Jay extended a brotherly handshake and claimed they had no beef and that it was just music. As we will see below, that is consistent with Jay's views about most rap beefs.

For Jay to tag Nas at the end of that blistering attack was the equivalent of laying down the gauntlet and then stomping it into the ground. Or, to shift metaphors, the beef between them had been fileted and seasoned and now it was ready to be sautéed.

Hot 97's Summer Jam has been a perennial platform for the hottest hip hop artists and the most salacious hip hop conflicts. But after that 2001 moment, I could not, in good conscience, join those who breathlessly awaited the next entry in what would be hip hop's greatest battle. I was at the time contemplating the lyrical life of Tupac. I was still in deep mourning for both Tupac and Biggie, two lyrical souls locked in mortal conflict. How could hip hop audiences gear up for another battle between hip hop legends? I knew that when titans battle, their minions go to war as well. Unless you have been to the Queensbridge Houses or the Marcy Projects, you might not be able to fully understand the grip of desperation that residential poverty has on its victims. You might not grasp how the lyrics from a champion of your hood might galvanize forces against his opponent's hood in ways that lead to unreported collateral damage. These rap battles are too often ratcheted up by media frenzy.

And so, for the "Takeover," and later, with Nas's response "Ether," I couldn't actually enjoy the artistry. I was unable to think of these exchanges as two verbal virtuosos trading well-organized modern versions of the dozens. For me, these were two mythological brothers at war with each other and hip hop culture hung in the balance. Hip hop could not survive a war between JAY-Z and Nas that moved off the records and into the streets. It was simply too soon.

My dark fears of the war between JAY-Z and Nas lightened in the aftermath of September 11, 2001. The world of hip hop seemed smaller in the face of the destruction, terror, and loss of human life that 9/11 projected across our television screens and seared into our imaginations. Like 9/11, the war between JAY-Z and Nas was ignited by actions and paradigm shifts that we didn't quite understand at that moment. When writers and thinkers return to the beef between JAY-Z and Nas now, they rarely fully engage the fear that cast a pall over the entire proceedings. Even for those who lauded the lyrical revival of Nas, or for those who eagerly chose their side in the bitter battle, it was fear of bloodshed that really underwrote hip hop's greatest war. It was clear then, even if it isn't now, that it wouldn't take much for the beef to turn into bullets.

What was ultimately at stake in this war of words was the lasting legacy of Notorious B.I.G., known even more colloquially as B.I.G. or Biggie Smalls. Biggie was murdered in a drive-by shooting in 1997 in Los Angeles on the eve of releasing his second and final album, *Life After Death*. Biggie and 2Pac had been caught in an ugly, tragic war of words. Their epic talent, and the hostilities encouraged by other figures, especially in Tupac's camp, framed their beef as a war between the East and West coasts. Sadly, careless coverage of the so-called coastal beef by segments of the hip hop media exacerbated the tense climate in which both Biggie and Tupac were brutally murdered.

Both Nas and Jay were close to Christopher Wallace. Biggie influenced and competed with them both. And when he was alive there was little question that Biggie was the king of New York rap. It was great sport for fans to debate who was better, supplying the name of whoever else may have been top of mind at the moment. But in the mid-nineties Wallace was so clearly the lyrical monarch of New York City rap that even Nas and Jay could agree on it. Vying for B.I.G.'s legacy was the natural trajectory for both men. Each had legitimate claim to it. Each had the requisite skills and borough bona fides to prosecute their claims effectively. After all, to be the king of New York rap is not only to inherit B.I.G.'s substantial crown, but to lay claim to ruling the broader cultural kingdom where hip hop began. At a certain point, things got ugly, super ugly in fact.

It is neither necessary nor helpful to rehash the drama of the "Super Ugly" phase of the JAY-Z–Nas rap war. "Super Ugly" was the second, more personal, more lethal installment of Jay's diss of Nas. It included the claim that Jay seduced Nas's baby's mother in their luxury car and left condoms on the infant seat. That fracas has sold enough magazines, funded enough radio ads, and generated enough clicks online for those who want to revisit that moment on their own. What makes "Super Ugly" the most important phase in this hip hop war was the singular intervention of JAY-Z's mother, Gloria Carter. A maternal touch transformed the tone and tenor of it all. She scolded her son for going too far in a rap battle that could have taken a far uglier turn than it did. Her scolding, and Jay's responsiveness to it, made hip hop better and, in fact, made JAY-Z a better man too. It didn't end the battle, but it reduced it to a respectable scuffle that ultimately ended in resolution, reconciliation, and collaboration. People talk about restorative justice and don't always know what it means. Gloria Carter restored justice to hip hop at one of its most critical junctures. And, most important, her son didn't lose his life in a senseless act of violence like his dear friend Christopher Wallace.

In "Moment of Clarity," from 2003's *The Black Album*, his first retirement record, Jay summarizes his legacy connection to the Notorious B.I.G. this way:

> *I'm strong enough to carry Biggie Smalls on my back*
> *And the whole BK, nigga, holla back.*

I use the term *legacy* here as an adjective, referring to software or hardware that is outdated but stays in use because it is pervasive and valuable. This is one of the best ways to appreciate JAY-Z's profound personal and professional ties to Biggie Smalls. But it is also a more effective way of wrestling with the notion that JAY-Z the artist, including his performances, music videos, books, tours, and lyrical acumen, is better than B.I.G. was. This is a tough pill to swallow for hip hop heads, and even for JAY-Z. You will never hear him in song or in an interview claim that he is better than his "brother" Biggie.

Sure, he laments lyrically from time to time that his

biggest competition is the unvanquished specter of two MCs whose legacies haunt him. In "Grammy Family Freestyle," in 2006, and then later on "Most Kingz," in 2010, Jay characterizes how he's viewed as an MC in comparison to his late friend, and his friend's rival, only to lament his own impossible dilemma.

> *Hov got flow though he's no Big and Pac, but he's close*
> *How I'm 'posed to win? They got me fightin' ghosts.*

The closest he has ever come to a claim of superiority is in a line from "Hola Hovito," where he opines, "And if I ain't better than Big, I'm the closest one."

That might have been the case at the time of *The Blueprint*'s release in 2001. But since then, Jay has expanded his lyrical and artistic corpus, adding eight more albums, including *Watch the Throne* with Kanye West. He has become a figure that in many ways transcends the culture of hip hop, amassing along the way a fan base and fortune that exponentially exceed that of his beloved brother from Brooklyn. Hip hop's reverence for Biggie Smalls is well placed, but nostalgia often clouds proper judgment. It is a legacy assessment to place Biggie over Jay on your Top Five list. We should acknowledge B.I.G.'s enduring place in the history of hip hop culture, his tragic and premature death, and his exceptionally canny approach to storytelling and narrative, the one area where he remains unrivaled. But in almost any other aspect of rhyming, and in every other aspect of performance, artistry, and industry success, Jay simply and categorically tops one of his best friends.

Twenty-two shots are fired on 1996's "Brooklyn's Finest," Jay and Biggie's first collaboration on record. The shots are blasted off before any lyrics are fired by these verbal impresarios from this storied borough of New York. There are at least a half dozen assaults with deadly weapons, retributive shootings, and robberies referenced in the song. Like JAY-Z's more recent urge to aggressive action on 2009's "D.O.A. (Death of Auto-Tune)," "Brooklyn's Finest" indeed, as Jay says on the former, "get[s] violent." The gunshots and the random referencing of clap backs, robberies, and kidnappings are more remarkable now than they were late in the last century. Gun violence on rap records in 1996 was more conventional than gun violence on rap records now. This is especially true for JAY-Z, who has evolved from his *Reasonable Doubt* days as a hungry MC with much to prove in an East Coast arena that still featured Nas, Wu-Tang Clan, and Biggie Smalls at their heights. You can hear hints of the competitive spirit between Biggie and Jay on "Brooklyn's Finest." They were both reformed hustlers, and the competition is about how ghoulish each MC can make their past seem in the rhetorical milieu.

The lyrical blueprint that Biggie lays down in his verses is instructive. "Brooklyn's Finest" isn't Jay and Big's only collaboration, but it is the most telling, because so much of what will happen to B.I.G., and how JAY-Z will eventually align himself as B.I.G.'s heir apparent, is built into these lyrics. Consider the following references in B.I.G.'s verses: "Frank White," the character in the 1990 cult flick *King of New York*; the phrase "Cristal forever"; the line "who shot ya?"; the word "warning"; and the line, "If Fay had twins, she probably have two Pacs (uh!) / Get it? Tu . . . Pac's."

The allusion to the film *King of New York* is the basis for the eventual contention that will erupt between Jay and Nas. Cristal definitely wasn't forever for hip hop culture, and it was JAY-Z, emerging from the shadow of B.I.G.'s legacy, who led the charge against Cristal for their racism in 2006. Hip hop frequently mentioned the high-end champagne in its songs for years. It often featured its trademark gold-labeled bottles in its music videos. But hip hoppers got a rude awakening when Frédéric Rouzaud, the managing director of the company that produces the bubbly, said that he viewed hip hop's affection for his brand with "curiosity and serenity." He said that while he couldn't "forbid people from buying it," he was "sure Dom Perignon or Krug would be delighted to have their business." Jay led the boycott of the company and eventually bought the champagne company Armand de Brignac, dubbed "Ace of Spades." Jay captured perfectly how social change often flows from personal experience on "Kingdom Come":

Fuck Cristal, so they ask me what we drinking
I thought dude's remark was rude okay
So I moved on to Dom, Krug Rosé
And it's much bigger issues in the world, I know
But I first had to take care of the world I know.

"Who Shot Ya?" and "Warning" are both breakout tracks on Biggie's 1994 classic debut, *Ready to Die*. But the phrase and word, along with the acerbically ironic reference to Tupac, are also eerily intermingled with the intangible yet volatile exchanges that fueled the so-called bicoastal rap feud. It is tragic and telling that both men's murders, one on a Las Vegas strip after a Mike Tyson fight, and the other on a popular Los Angeles nightlife strip after a *Vibe* magazine party, remain unsolved.

And yet for all the gunshots and threats that ring through this energetic collaboration between Jay and B.I.G., the lines that ultimately carry the most weight, the words that have the most potential to haunt listeners even now, are the lyrics directed at Biggie's wife, the R&B singer Faith Evans. Tupac claimed on record that he had a sexual encounter with Faith, a claim she vehemently denied. Given the tensions of the time, I believe Faith without question; I did then, I do now. But the fact that Faith became the instrument through which the beef between Biggie and Tupac was deepened is one of the saddest and most misogynistic moments of this dark phase in hip hop's short history. The most vicious exchanges between these two men came at the expense of an innocent woman. Referencing rumors of a relationship between his wife and Tupac, Biggie let loose on "Brooklyn's Finest": "If Fay had twins, she'd probably have two Pacs (uh!) / Get it? Tu . . . Pac's?" Two weeks later, Pac responded with a vile onslaught on his song "Hit 'Em Up," saying in the spoken intro to the song: "I ain't got no motherfuckin' friends / That's why I fucked yo' bitch, you fat motherfucker!" Then he spoke venom in verse:

> *First off, fuck yo' bitch and the clique you claim*
> *Westside when we ride, come equipped with game*
> *You claim to be a player, but I fucked your wife*
> *We bust on Bad Boys, niggas fucked for life.*

The words ring shamefully in our ears now even if they did not do so then. It is especially tragic that Christopher Wallace and Tupac Shakur didn't get the opportunity to mature as men and find their way past the abhorrent visions of masculinity that imprisoned them both as young men. Thank God that Shawn Carter was given more time and space to work through his own views of women and relationships in a way denied these other two lyrical legends. Jay also would have many more beefs, mostly inconsequential skirmishes, but they were instructive both for their lack of violence and for showing how one can disagree, and be quite disagreeable, at first, before finding one's way to peace.

In a 2002 interview with radio personality Angie Martinez, while still embroiled in a very public war of words with Nas, JAY-Z explained the rationale behind most benign rap beefs. "People clash at the top," Jay said, echoing Nas's line on his 1999 song "We Will Survive," where, speaking directly to the late 2Pac, Nas confessed they "had words 'cause the best supposed to clash at the top." Jay continued: "I'm number one, you wanna be number one. You feel you number one, I wanna be number one. Let's do it." Jay implored the audience not to "believe these guys when they be talking tough." Jay summed up hip hop conflict in two words. "It's wrestling."

He drew on his own experience for an example. In 1999, then unsigned rapper 50 Cent had a radio hit, "How to Rob," where he boasted he would perpetrate thievery on Jay. Jay retorted with a caustic couplet on "It's Hot (Some Like It Hot)" in 1999 at that year's Summer Jam.

> *Go against Jigga your ass is dense*
> *I'm about a dollar, what the fuck is 50 Cents?*

Jay told Martinez that before his performance, backstage, he said to 50 that "I respect the record, yeah I liked that record, it was hot. But you know I gotta spank you dog." "No doubt, do your thing," 50 told Jay. "Then it was peace," Jay says. "History." Although they've traded barbs since, their minor conflict never threatened to bleed into the streets. WWE for certain.

Jay referenced the tiff on 2009's "A Star Is Born," a song at once praising gifted newcomers and applauding those who left their mark on the rap game since Jay started, many of whom had fallen off, proving Jay's staying power as he bragged,

> *I am one of one*
> *Can't you see just how long my run?*

Jay said of the newest rap phenom, "Drake's up next, see what he do with it." Jay realizes that rap is "a young man's sport," as he told *New York Times* executive editor Dean Baquet, that the "white hot space" of artistic creativity belongs to those who are hungry to exult in clever cadence and mesmerizing meter, a spot he occupied for a long spell. But Jay knows that there is something greater, something deeper than immense popularity: staying power that trumps musical trends. He is enormously wealthy and influential today because he has been for a long time a cultural giant who divines the zeitgeist through a microphone. Several decades later he remains in utter command of his craft.

Yet, at times, he has been willing to acknowledge gifted heirs to the throne. His generosity, it must be noted, grew from supreme confidence. Jay's unquenchable competitive fire is matched only by his unshakable belief that he holds the most revered spot in the pantheon of hip hop greats. If you're the G.O.A.T., no need to be worried about the B.U.C.K., Best Undisputed Current King. Jay put in a stirring guest appearance on New Orleans–bred rapper Lil Wayne's "Mr. Carter," playing on both their surnames, on the younger rapper's most celebrated album, 2008's *Tha Carter III*. Lil Wayne was then in the white hot space of acclaim as the next greatest rapper alive, and Jay encouraged him to take, without apology, his rightful place at the top, which he had earned through electrifying elocution. The point, after all, is to be the best.

> *I'm right here in my chair with my crown and my*
> *dear*
> *Queen B, as I share, mic time with my heir*
> *Young Carter, go farther, go further, go harder*
> *Is that not why we came? And if not, then why*
> *bother?*

Lil Wayne was a verbal savant whose eccentric intellection and idiosyncratic Weltanschauung burned brightly in mixtapes and albums, but then flamed out a bit, or at least got doused, in an extended battle with his record label.

In the meantime, Wayne's protégé Drake dominated the marketplace and proved to have epic cultural reach, in large measure because he reinvigorated the emotional register of rap. Jay's relationship with Drake has been more complicated than that with Wayne. That is partly because Drake rose higher and has stayed longer than Wayne. It is also because Drake, despite calling Jay on

Hot 97 in 2013 "an incredible mentor," has taken louder shots at the throne than Wayne, mostly about Jay (and Kanye) falling off, or Jay's increasing reference to art in his lyrics. "It's like Hov can't drop bars these days without at least four art references! I would love to collect at some point, but I think the whole rap/art world thing is getting kind of corny," Drake told *Rolling Stone* in February 2014. Jay fired back a month later on rapper Jay Electronica's remix to "We Made It":

> *Sorry Mrs. Drizzy for so much art talk*
> *Silly me rappin' 'bout shit that I really bought*
> *While these rappers rap about guns they ain't shot*
> *And a bunch of other silly shit that they ain't got.*

Drake hit back a week later on the song "Draft Day": "I'm focused on making records and gettin' bigger / Just hits, no misses, that's for the married folk," cleverly parrying Jay's feminization of him, a classic dozens, and sexist, gesture in hip hop. Not to be outdone, Jay fired back on DJ Khaled's "They Don't Love You No More":

> *Niggas talking down on the crown*
> *Watch them niggas you 'round got you wound*
> *Haters wanna ball, let me tighten up my drawstring*
> *Wrong sport, boy, you know you as soft as a lacrosse*
> *   team.*

Back and forth they went a few more times, never producing anything vicious, never anything that appeared to be more than sparring between two heavyweights, and along the way Jay even recorded two more songs with Drake, including one on Drake's 2018 album, *Scorpion*.

Jay retained his respect and admiration for Drake despite their benign conflicts. But Jay's crack on Drake's "softness" reflected a charge made since the start of the younger artist's career. Ironically, Drake, a figure known for his emotional intensity—and for his fearlessness in embracing his "female" energy while avoiding the relentless misogyny that plagues the genre—has also drawn derision and scorn, including from female fans of hip hop. It's no surprise that Drake has been tagged as "soft" by zealots of hardcore hip hop. The genre is famously combative and thrives on Oedipal conflicts and stylish fratricide. Drake "hate"—of course not all criticism is hate, but a lot of the grousing about Drake certainly qualifies—is stoked by flawed ideas of ghetto authenticity and manhood. The prisoners of racial claustrophobia see Drake as a goofy black man who isn't "real" because he's a biracial ex–teen television star from Toronto. But those who entertain a broader view of blackness welcome Drake as a fellow traveler.

Even ardent fans are weary of hardcore artists flashing receipts for a cartoonish masculinity that few can afford to buy. Such flagrantly archaic views of manhood beg a fundamental question: Can that many "bitches" have riled that many "niggas" in the Maybach on the way to the club to pop collars and bottles before having empty sex and killing foes who offend their honor? It's easy to lose count, and accountability, of the bodies. Drake deserves high praise for breaking the thug logjam in hip hop and pushing past brute machismo to embrace masculine vulnerability. That may be the shining core of Drake hate: he amplifies his emotions as eloquently as he speaks his mind. Too many rap artists carry their feelings like a concealed weapon while Drake shoots from the left side of his chest right into the nearest microphone.

"The game needed life, I put my heart in it," Drake raps on "The Resistance," lamenting on the song's hook how the success he pined for now keeps him from loved ones: "What am I afraid of? This is supposed to be what dreams are made of." On "Own It," Drake reverses gender roles and pleads for intimacy: instead of sex, he wants to "make love / Next time we talk, I don't wanna just talk, I wanna trust." On the infectious mid-tempo stepper "Hold On, We're Going Home," rumored to be about on-again, off-again flame Rihanna, Drake confesses, "I can't get over you / You left your mark on me." Drake in these songs and in much of his oeuvre violates a cardinal rule in hip hop: when it comes to women, never let them see you fret.

Drake's emotional transparency isn't all that has sparked ire; his rhymes are often awash in melodies that cascade from a pleasant tenor singing voice, a feat that supposedly angers rap gods, who frown on the mingling of hip hop and rhythm and blues. Other great artists like Lauryn Hill and CeeLo Green have brilliantly rapped and sung on their respective releases. But no one in rap has ever done so as effectively as Drake, giving fresh definition to b-boy, or break-boy. He not only sings his own hooks, and sings his own songs, but breaks into song in the middle of a rap, and vice versa. Or he alternates between rapping and singing in the same line, or sometimes in the same phrase, thus breaking down the barrier between acts of speech and song and making quite nervous those intent on keeping them discrete enterprises. Drake's sonic hybridity, his fusion of speech and song, mirrors his hybridity of race and place as an artist with a white mother from Canada and a black father from the United States.

The alienation from Drake by emotionally immature men has been matched by a surprisingly negative female reaction to the crooner-rapper. To be sure, this isn't a scientific survey, but one drawn from anecdotes, and my evidence was collected in an informal poll of women across the country (clearly not the thousands of screaming ladies I see at Drake's concerts) who are stumped by my affection for the self-described "light-skinned Keith Sweat," and who find Drake intolerably self-reflective, melancholy, and emotional. It is difficult to hear such critiques when the urban version of the strong, silent type offers little comfort or support to women. That type often appears to be Hercules in sagging pants with low emotional intelligence.

The effort of many women to awaken men to the emotional currents around them suggests that such "sensitivity" is a quality they find desirable. The catty memes of Drake posted by women in social media gibing the artist for his emotional makeup amplify the distorted romantic images and expectations that engulf a generation of women inured to poor treatment by their men. The shame isn't Drake's; the shame is that we can't endorse a black man who isn't a thug and who wears his heart on his sleeve. On his masterly *4:44* Jay embraced an even more honest and redemptive emotional vulnerability than what has been touted by Drake.

Although it appears that Drake and Jay are far apart when it comes to visual art, there are signs the fine arts ice between them is melting. There is Drake's heavy reference to light-magic visual artist James Turrell on his massive 2015 hit "Hotline Bling." And on Drake's turn at the mic on rapper Meek Mill's 2018 "Going Bad" (the result of them resolving their beef to record together), he says, "Yeah, lot of Murakami in the hallway (What?)." (Takashi Murakami is a Japanese contemporary fine arts and commercial media artist who has designed album covers for Kanye West, and who has collaborated with Drake on designer jackets and other fashion items.) While Drake appears to be dipping his toes in the fine arts waters, Jay has clearly been baptized in its healing streams.

Art has been historically viewed as too highbrow for the black masses. Art galleries, art exhibitions, and most art museums have largely ignored or refused to cater to black communities starved of images and art that reflect their culture and their spiritual and moral yearnings. Tina Knowles-Lawson, Beyoncé's mother, saw the value in art as a young woman and filled her home with images of black folk. "When my kids were growing up, it was really important to me that they saw images of African-Americans," Lawson told *Vanity Fair* magazine in 2018. "I'm so happy that I did, because both of them are really aware of their culture, and I think a lot of that had to do with looking at those images every day, those strong images." It is clearly a lesson that her son-in-law Jay has absorbed over the years.

In fact, the failure of the art world to accommodate black identity and to affirm norms and standards of black beauty inspired JAY-Z in 2011 to conjure a gallery of black and brown female icons worthy of curation:

> *I mean Marilyn Monroe, she's quite nice*
> *But why all the pretty icons always all white?*
> *Put some colored girls in the MoMA*
> *Half these broads ain't got nothing on Willona*

Don't make me bring Thelma in it
Bring Halle, bring Penélope and Salma in it
Back to my Beyoncés
You deserve three stacks, word to André
Call Larry Gagosian, you belong in museums

To be sure it wasn't just black females who deserved a place on the museum wall. JAY-Z found a way to insert his black body into the conversation. Officially listed as "A Performance Art Film," the nearly eleven-minute video for JAY-Z's 2013 song "Picasso Baby" is an ode to New York's multicultural landscape. In it, he cites artists and also offers a verbal rebuff to persistent racism and the relentless scrutiny of his iconic status. The song's video was given cinematic treatment when it debuted on the cable television channel HBO in August 2013. The video was filmed in July 2013 at New York's Pace Gallery.

"Picasso Baby" is a visual gallery of Jay's understanding of how he became the artist he is today. In the last third of the song, and midway through the film, the ebullient production of "Picasso Baby" breaks down to a grittier affair with guitar riffs and a throwback backbeat. Here the song, and JAY-Z's performance of it before a live audience, shifts into its hardest "self." Up until this point, "Picasso Baby" is the usual aspirational and materialistic fare with artistic shout-outs and clever references to "fine" art and artists: Picasso, Mona Lisa, marble floors, gold ceilings, MoMA, Warhol, Art Basel, Leonardo da

Vinci, and the Met. And of course there is a reference to Jean-Michel Basquiat, the gifted black neo-expressionist artist whose work inspired JAY-Z as it probed "suggestive dichotomies" like wealth versus poverty, integration versus segregation, inner perception versus outer experience. But once the break intervenes, both the song and the film assume a more intense, and purposeful, tone.

Now Jay motions the surrounding crowd closer to him. The invitation suggests that proximity might enhance the experience as the artist delves into a deeper form of expression. In the earlier portion of the performance Jay is cordoned off in the center of the gallery, as if he is a work of art himself. His performance art film pays direct homage to the legendary Marina Abramović, the Serbian-born sensation who has shaken and shaped the art world with her fearless, and at times violent, performance art pieces. Abramović's 2010 "The Artist Is Present" is a masterly show of endurance and artistic exploration built on Abramović's commitment to sit silently for over 700 hours and look into the eyes of those who gaze upon her performance. Abramović's body of work quite literally, limb by limb, her flesh as the canvas, forms an improbable bridge between her status in the art world, and JAY-Z's extraordinary journey from the Marcy Projects to the heights of the world of art. It all culminated, in a way, with JAY-Z's six-hour performance art piece in the Chelsea Pace Gallery in July 2013, which was distilled to his eleven-minute video. Abramović's willingness to put her body on the line is not something with which JAY-Z was unfamiliar. He did so himself, repeatedly, willingly, hustling on the dangerous streets in pursuit of material gain. But that was JAY-Z the blight hustler. JAY-Z the bright hustler, the artist, now uses those experiences to enjoy a measure of success he could scarcely have begun to imagine when he was dealing drugs on the block.

But the break in the film, and in the song, is a cue to take us back to *that* JAY-Z, and to situate this performance art film in the annals of the fine art forms that embrace and embody sacrifice. Attacks from the media, disgruntled fans, annoying paparazzi, and run-ins with the law form the underside of success and fame. It is a theme that regularly recurs in Jay's body of work. In frustration JAY-Z glares into the camera for full effect. "I put down the cans and they ran amok," he nearly screams— and here cans are at least a triple entendre of spray paint cans for graffiti, pistols, and headphones—as he pantomimes shooting his enemies with a gun in each hand. His next lines gesture toward the visceral damage that bullets cause the human body, linking him to the film's Serbian muse and to his not-so-distant past as a drug dealer. There's more shooting before this verse concludes as Jay recalls his "cans" metaphor to slip in another allusion to Basquiat, claiming that he will "spray everything like SAMO"—the graffiti duo Basquiat was a part of that scrawled esoteric epigrams all over Lower East Side

Manhattan buildings in the late seventies. Although it is not the final line, Jay's reminder, "Don't forget, America, this how you made me," punctuates the song and the performance in a way that only an underprivileged son of urban America could. It puts a period on a performance art piece in one of the most elite artistic spaces in the world.

The "Picasso Baby" performance art film reflects JAY-Z's sustained engagement with fine art. In his "Blue Magic" video from 2007, Jay raps in front of a painting by Takashi Murakami (yes, the same artist Drake has teamed with) and spin-art skull paintings by British artist, collector, and entrepreneur Damien Hirst. In his 2008 Glastonbury music festival performance, Jay rapped before a visual backdrop that featured Hirst's diamond-encrusted skull entitled "For the Love of God." A couple of years later a replica of the skull was made and can be seen throughout Jay's 2010 video for his song "On to the Next One." (Although controversy has dogged Hirst's art since 1999 with charges of plagiarism, his preoccupation with death resonates with elements of hip hop culture that address carnage, suffering, and mortality.) In his verse on Rick Ross's 2008 song "Maybach Music," Jay shows how his artistic register has expanded.

> *The curtains are drawn*
> *perfectly like a Picasso, Rembrandts and Rothkos*
> *I'm a major player, 40/40's in Vegas at the Palazzo.*

It's the same year he was spotted with Beyoncé attending the international contemporary art fair Art Basel Miami Beach, and a year before he told the *Mirror* that he owned pieces by Hirst and Richard Prince. In 2009, Jay also compared himself to a Warhol painting on "Already Home":

> *I'm in The Hall already, on the wall already*
> *I'm a work of art, I'm a Warhol already.*

It's the same year he bragged on "Off That" that he was "In my TriBeCa loft / With my highbrow art and my high yellow broad."

In 2011, on "Who Gon Stop Me," a duet with Kanye, Jay added the Museum of Modern Art to his list of artistic allusions.

> *Pablo Picasso, Rothkos, Rilkes*
> *Graduated to the MoMA*
> *And I did all of this without a diploma.*

The cover art for his 2011 memoir, *Decoded*, was designed by graphic artist Rodrigo Corral and features a gold-embossed version of Andy Warhol's "Rorschach." In his classic 2006 collaboration with Lupe Fiasco, "Pressure," on Fiasco's debut album, Jay name-checks Warhol.

> *If the war calls for Warhols*
> *Hope you got enough space on your hall's walls.*

On "Ain't I," a track that was likely recorded as early as 2006 but wasn't released until 2008 on DJ Clue?'s *Desert Storm Radio Volume 8* mixtape, Jay raps that

> *I got Warhols on my hall's wall*
> *I got Basquiats in the lobby of my spot*

His affinity for Warhol is understandable: Warhol reshaped the gateways to the fine arts world by unapologetically embracing a pop art aesthetic and relentlessly sampling and remaking popular culture as fine art, aesthetic features that made him interesting and inspiring for the young Jean-Michel Basquiat.

While the fine arts captured Jay's attention, he was also captivated by popular art in elite settings. If we had to choose one single that catapulted JAY-Z from stardom to superstardom it would have to be "Hard Knock Life (Ghetto Anthem)," from his third album, *Vol. 2*, released in 1998. That album sold over five million copies in the United States. The single was instrumental in propelling that record to five-times-platinum status back when fans still purchased CDs from actual brick-and-mortar music stores. "Hard Knock Life" interpolates a refrain from the song "It's the Hard Knock Life," featured in the Broadway musical *Annie*. A Broadway musical, if not quite fine art, was nevertheless viewed as finer art than hip hop by many of Broadway's patrons. The sampling of the song was also a nod to Jay's openness to a variety of art forms and his understanding that common themes of existential struggle unite disparate genres of music. Thus one of his most successful songs, at a critical point in his career, features a sample from a Broadway musical that highlights the plight of poor, socially invisible children. *Vol. 2* won the Grammy for Best Rap Album that year. Jay's song, the sample of the original, the themes of the musical in which the original song was performed, and the acknowledgment from the Recording Academy all form a Warholian narrative, a pastiche of key pop cultural moments.

And yet, while Warhol is undeniably an artistic touchstone, JAY-Z identifies far more intensely with the Brooklyn-born fine artist Jean-Michel Basquiat. In *Decoded* and elsewhere Jay discusses how Basquiat's 1982 painting "Charles the First"—featuring the artist's rendering of jazz saxophonist Charlie Parker with textual inscriptions about the god Thor that elevate Parker to mythical stature—inspired his 2010 song "Most Kingz," produced by DJ Green Lantern and featuring Coldplay front man Chris Martin. For Jay, Basquiat's "Charles the First" is a visual treatise on the perils and pitfalls of success. "Success is like suicide," he claims on the track. The track where Martin sings the hook functions as the auditory leitmotif, the spoken complement to Basquiat's raw textual interventions in the painting: "Most kings get their heads cut off." Basquiat was likely alluding to the late great Charlie Parker, who, like Basquiat himself, died early from a drug overdose. Like Basquiat, and Jay, Parker contended with a white world that eventually embraced his art even as he continued to face racism. It was tough to survive in such a world, one that drove both Basquiat and Parker to taking drugs, and Jay earlier to selling them.

Jay doesn't take his survival lightly. "Most Kingz" gives a litany of those, like Martin Luther King, Jr., Malcolm X, and even Pac and Biggie, who achieved fame and died well before their time. His purchase of art, besides its aesthetic, financial, and political value, may possess a compelling existential one, too: it is a way of keeping alive the legacy of black men who blazed the path before him. In 2013, Jay paid $4.5 million to acquire Basquiat's "Mecca" at Sotheby's in Manhattan. With the exception of B.I.G., Jay alludes to Basquiat more than any other artist. In a standout line in "Picasso Baby," he claims:

It ain't hard to tell
I'm the new Jean Michel

And in some ways, he is a new, longer-living version of the legendary Basquiat: born nearly a decade apart, both are black prodigies, both became global icons, both fought to have their art taken seriously by the world.

But the first line, usually overlooked when this verse is cited, is similarly allusive and just as powerful. It's a quote from the 1994 song "It Ain't Hard to Tell," from *Illmatic*, the classic debut album of Nas, another rap genius. It shows how JAY-Z continues to appreciate the art forms that nurtured his own gift. But it shows, too, how Jay reconciles artistically what he has reconciled personally, and that by alluding to one of Nas's most famous songs, he has found peace and brotherhood with a former rival. And it means something even more important: that, at least rhetorically, perhaps even literally, he kept at least two kings' heads, Nas's and his own, from being cut off. That may be one of Jay's most generous if greatly unappreciated gestures.

If Jay has tangled in verse with icons like Nas and Drake, and if he has cited the lives of fallen icons like Basquiat and Parker, King and Malcolm, he has also occasionally explored the appeal and relevance of another iconic figure: the comic book superhero. Indeed, hip hop has a long-standing love affair with superheroes, in part because of their similar quest for social justice. The relationship is also fed by the belief that rappers and superheroes both overcome enormous odds to represent their communities on the largest platforms possible. It wouldn't be an exaggeration to say that rappers are superheroes for many of the folk in the communities they come from. It makes sense that hip hop artists often turn to comics and superhero genres to make important points about love, the hood, crime, poverty, and, in the case of JAY-Z on *Kingdom Come*, the music industry itself.

Kingdom Come takes its title from a popular comic book miniseries of the same name. In DC's 1996 version of *Kingdom Come,* traditional superheroes like Superman and Wonder Woman have receded from public life and left the work of world-saving and fighting bad guys to a new breed of hero. In this world, traditional superheroes are out of touch with reality and disconnected from the goings-on in the streets. Therefore, just as JAY-Z did in the music industry, these heroes retire. In their place rises a new hero, named Magog. He is of an utterly different ethical order. For Magog the ends always justify the means; he kills and destroys to save, serve, and protect. The results are disastrous, and the traditional superheroes, especially Wonder Woman, plead for Superman to come out of retirement. Superman finally agrees and comes back to better the dystopic world that Magog has created.

Jay's microphone went silent, symbolically, in 2003 after the release of *The Black Album*, one of the top three records of his career. In the three years of his retirement, the music, production, and lyrical aesthetics of hip hop shifted regions, altered themes, and, too often, dipped in artistic skills. 2006 saw artists like Chingy ("Pullin' Me Back"), Young Dro ("Shoulder Lean"), Yung Joc ("It's Goin' Down"), T.I. ("What You Know"), and Dem Franchize Boyz ("Lean Wit It, Rock Wit It") take center stage in hip hop. Between 2003 and 2006 the mainstream rap music industry took a turn toward trap musical production—which is bass heavy and features rapid-fire high hats, glowing in Southern drug dealer chic—and what some critics cynically refer to as "mumble rap," a trend so dominant that it thrives in the present moment.

In this sense, *Kingdom Come* is a comeback album that plays as an extended superhero comic book analogy. Jay represents those traditional heroes who have receded in retirement only to see the culture that they spent their careers cultivating squandered in the hands of a new crop of rappers and heroes with a different set of artistic and moral standards. If we push this comparison further, we can understand the monumental significance of Jay's collaboration with former N.W.A (Niggaz Wit Attitudes) member and seminal producer Dr. Dre on this record. Dre produced "Lost One," "30 Something," "Trouble," and "Minority Report." A mere decade earlier such an extensive collaboration was unimaginable. (Although Jay had in 1999 supplied the words for Dre's influential hit "Still D.R.E.") And much like Jay, Dre was coming to terms with the changing paradigms of the culture. In Dre's case it was musical production shifting away from the aesthetic conventions and musical vocabulary he was familiar with, especially the G-funk sound of throbbing bass, melodic synthesizers, live instrumentation, dense harmonies, and sprightly chord progressions that reigned on the West Coast during the "golden era" of hip hop from 1988 to 1998.

"Kingdom Come," the title track, features a variety of iconic and superhero allusions, including Superman and

Clark Kent, Spiderman and Peter Parker, Iceberg Slim, Underdog, and Flash Gordon.

> *Just when they thought it was all over*
> *I put the whole world on my back and broad*
>   *shoulders*
> *The boy HOVA, who you know talk all over tracks*
>   *like that?*
> *Guess what New York, New York—we back!*

Themes of retirement, heroics, and the savior's return in "Kingdom Come" are emblematic of the moment. They resonate throughout the rest of the record, putting each track in the context of rap music's paradigmatic shifts and the angst felt by aging hip hop impresarios as the reins of the culture seemed to be slipping from their grasp.

Kingdom Come is widely considered, even by the artist himself, to be JAY-Z's weakest album. Jay and the critics couldn't be more wrong. *Kingdom Come* is one of his most accomplished and mature albums—*4:44*'s prelude in some ways. Jay seriously considered releasing *Kingdom Come* under his "government name." And maybe history will categorize this record and *4:44* as the Shawn Carter albums within JAY-Z's full body of work. If *Kingdom Come* is his worst effort, then how do we account for the palpable pain expressed at losing his nephew Colleek in an automobile accident, and feeling partly responsible for his death, on "Lost One"?

My nephew died in the car I bought
So I'm under the belief it's partly my fault
Close my eyes and squeeze, try to block that thought
Place any burden on me but please, not that, Lord
But time don't go back, it goes forward
Can't run from the pain, go towards it
Some things can't be explained, what caused it?
Such a beautiful soul, so pure, shit!

How does one account for the dreamy existential reflections on destiny, his nephew in heaven, karma, and the consequences to his unborn daughters in "Beach Chair":

Colleek, are you praying for me?
See I got demons in my past, so I got daughters on
    the way
If the prophecy's correct, then the child should have
    to pay
For the sins of a father
So I barter my tomorrows against my yesterdays
In hope that she'll be okay

What of his unsparing self-examination and advocacy for social justice on "Minority Report," which I'll explore at length in the next chapter? And "The Prelude" is likely the best opening of any hip hop album of that era, where Jay gets back at rival rappers, does an autopsy on the hip hop game, and announces that at thirty-seven, and coming out of retirement, he is still king of the hill:

> *Woo! Guess who's back?*
> *Since this is a New Era, got a fresh new hat*
> *Ten year veteran, I've been set*
> *I've been through with this bullshit game but I*
>   *never can*
> *I used to think rappin' at 38 was ill*
> *Well last year alone I grossed 38 mill'*
> *I know I ain't quite 38 but still*
> *The flow so Special got a .38 feel*
> *The real is back.*

Kingdom Come is a decidedly adult album with mature themes. If hip hop is becoming "lil," and "young," *Kingdom Come* is all grown up. It does many of the things that make Jay a powerful poet and influential intellectual: it alludes to pop cultural moments and figures, reflects on aging, rampages through metaphors, tropes, and double entendres, fights the powers that be, addresses urban crises, beefs a bit, mourns loss in elegiac gestures, proclaims his greatness in eloquent verse, embraces his mother's love, thinks out loud about fame's costs, and probes the ethereal, transcendent nature of human identity and destiny.

The album was panned by critics, at least in part because Jay wasn't exclusively, or primarily, rapping about hustling. (Maybe the critics skimmed through the hustler's itinerary performed con brio as Jay's narrator brags he "brought that crack back like a yo-yo" and lamented "all these rival dealers trying to do me in" on "Oh My God.") That said, JAY-Z did follow *Kingdom Come* with *American Gangster*, considered a return to form by critics and his core fan base alike. It is a great record, but so is *Kingdom Come*. In fact, what *Here, My Dear* was to Marvin Gaye, *Kingdom Come* is to Jay: an underappreciated record that was far greater than its critical reception suggested at the time. But to match the naked self-revelation and brutal honesty that Gaye managed on *Here, My Dear*, Jay would have to dig deeper into his life and look deeper into his soul. Jay would soon discover, more than ever before, the wisdom of the feminist credo: the personal is political.

Black women have shouldered so much of the weight and the responsibility for the challenges that Black folks face in relationships. And we have endured 40 years of angry Black men in hip hop telling us that it is all our fault. JAY-Z provides an important corrective to this narrative, and he opens the door for a different kind of cultural conversation . . . Hip hop owes it to Black men to allow them to be more complex and complicated characters than the caricatures of toughness and insensitivity that they often become in popular culture.

BRITTNEY COOPER

Dualities exist in JAY-Z's career-wide embrace of crass consumerism and his critique of how elite establishment powers that be keep their foot on the neck of the underclass. The complexity of this duality is at the core of his political philosophy. In that, JAY-Z is transcending the status quo.

BAKARI KITWANA

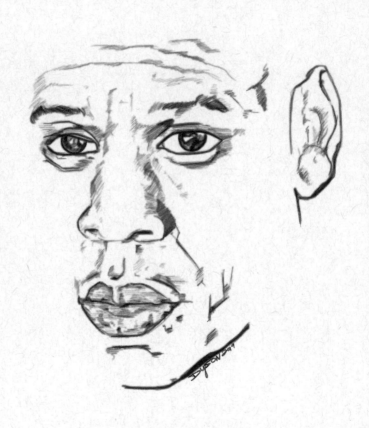

"Somewhere in America"

POLITICS

While it is true that JAY-Z has matured politically over the years, his obsession with hustling and his unabashed capitalist aspirations may have blunted our appreciation for how "woke" he's been from the start. Hustling, as we have seen, not only has moral consequences, but it has myriad social and political meanings as well. JAY-Z has been an eagle-eyed social critic who has commented in his lyrics on pressing issues, and there is a lot he has taken stock of. The misuse of psychotherapy and the overmedication of black youth. The politics of black masculinity and the politics of black love. Racial injustice and the impact of slavery on contemporary culture. European misadventures in colonialism and American myths of patriotism and empire. Police brutality and 9/11 and its relation to black folk.

JAY-Z has also addressed the racial context of natural disasters and their exposure of political hypocrisy. He has taken on criminal justice reform. And he has offered invaluable criticism of civil rights icons, allowing us to grapple with the moral contradictions of black elites in entertainment and leadership. He has proved along the way that hip hop is a way to say the words that matter the most to our moral advance. As is the case with many Negro spirituals, political meaning is often hidden in the lyrics, crammed between the lines, or tucked away in songs that are lesser hits so that their meaning takes, well, fewer hits—lest those surveilling the content identify its liberating or subversive intent. That may mean that some quarters of conservative or respectable black America overlook or ignore those messages too. Jay evokes this double meaning skillfully. "It's like a old negro spiritual, but I mastered Toby," he says on "Some People Hate," referring to the character in the book and TV series *Roots* who is stolen from Africa with the name Kunta Kinte but given the name Toby when enslaved in America.

A major reason looms for misinterpreting JAY-Z's political pedigree: his highly visible role in a dramatic period of American history has obscured his prior political engagement. Barack Obama and JAY-Z had effortless simpatico and irresistible appeal as giants who saw pieces of themselves in each other. The Obama connection was sexy and tailor-made for the papers and the digital sphere that took a shine to their productive partnership.

Obama was a wunderkind who seemed to emerge fully formed, like Athena out of some political Zeus's head, in 2004 to join the United States Senate, only to ascend to the presidency a mere four years later. Before his rise he was a local politician who labored in relative obscurity as an Illinois state representative. If we compare him to JAY-Z, Obama's time in the state legislature was like the time Jay spent hustling in the streets while searching for a record deal. Obama's failure in a 2000 election to unseat former Black Panther Bobby Rush as a congressman is comparable to Jay getting turned down time and again by music executives before he founded his own label and released his first album in 1996.

The similarities don't end there. Obama and Jay are both tall, talented, and tremendously charismatic men who used words to forge their paths in the world. Both are the definition of black cool. Levelheaded Afropolitans, they exhibit black grace under white pressure, pivoting in the black world and navigating through the white one, their complicated identities remaining intact. Obama, of course, absorbed and reproduced a bivalent racial identity, filtering his whiteness through his black eyes, discovering the meaning of his blackness in the presence of whiter bodies. Jay's blackness was equally bisected, though his experience of race intersected not with color but with class. The black poor may as well have been foreigners, so wide was the gulf between Marcy and the upper reaches of black Manhattan. Both Obama and Jay endured troubled paternity. Their black fathers made indecent and soul-shearing exits, briefly returning, only to be gone for good. It seems that JAY-Z forgave his father in a way that Obama could not. Perhaps that is because Jay got the sort of closure never afforded Obama. After all, Obama last saw his father when he was an unformed boy of ten (even though his father didn't die until Obama was twenty-one), which is far different than seeing your father for the final time at thirty-three, when you've ascended to superstardom, as Jay did. However, previous to that, JAY-Z hadn't seen his father since he was eleven, and his father died shortly after they reconnected.

Obama and Jay are both married to strong and brilliant women whose popularity outstrips their own. Obama said as he offered tribute to Jay by video for the Songwriters Hall of Fame ceremony in 2017 that he had been listening to the rapper since he was a "young and hungry state senator." He sampled Jay during his 2008 presidential campaign against Hillary Clinton when he symbolically brushed the dirt off his shoulders, signifying that her attacks on him were easily discarded, mimicking a move made in the video for JAY-Z's "Dirt Off Your Shoulder." He tweeted a reference to Jay's "My 1st Song" from his *Black Album* (a song stressing that one should treat one's last song like one's first, one's first like one's last, staying hungry and putting one's heart into the effort) while adding the finishing touches on his last State of the Union Address. Jay's words on his supposed swan song before retirement in 2003 inspired Obama as he faced the end of his office.

> *It's my life—it's my pain and my struggle*
> *The song that I sing to you it's my ev-ery-thing*
> *Treat my first like my last, and my last like my first*
> *And my thirst is the same as when I came*
> *It's my joy and my tears and the laughter it brings*
>   *to me*
> *It's my ev-ery-thing.*

Obama bragged in his tribute, "I'm pretty sure I'm still the only president to listen to JAY-Z's music in the Oval Office."

Jay was equally taken by Obama, campaigning for him during both presidential runs, often joined by Beyoncé, and raising big money. (Obama tweeted a photo of a smiling trio—him, Jay, and Beyoncé—a month before his 2012 reelection, with the caption, "A couple supporters in a New York State of mind last night.") Jay made campaign ads for Obama, and, of course, he joined Young Jeezy and Nas on the remix to "My President Is Black," and, in a live performance of the song in Washington, D.C., on the eve of Obama's inauguration, he humorously suggested that racists might even find some relief in Obama's white heritage.

My president is black
In fact he's half white
So even in a racist mind
He's half right
If you have a racist mind
You be aight.

Jay also tweaked an anonymous poem that was widely circulated on the Internet in 2008. The poem was based on a February 2008 speech by former Louisiana congressman Cleo Fields, who said that "W.E.B. DuBois taught so that Rosa Parks could take a seat. Rosa took a seat so we all could take a stand. We all took a stand so that Martin Luther King, Jr., could march. Martin marched so Jesse Jackson could run. Jesse ran so Obama could WIN." Scholar DuBois and civil rights leader Jackson, two of our most important icons, were removed in the popular online poem. Jay rapped that "Rosa Parks sat so Martin Luther could walk / Martin Luther walked so Barack Obama could run," which Obama in turn paraphrased in his 2015 speech at the fiftieth anniversary celebration of the Selma march. "We honored those who walked so we could run. We must run so our children soar."

Many mistakenly believe that JAY-Z's first extensive foray into establishment politics was the only time he talked about issues he cared for. Beyond his support of Obama, Jay has also mastered a sneak-and-speak approach to political commentary. He laces his lyrics with pieces of social and political insight, from entire blocs of songs, to extended metaphors, to just a word or two. On "Made in America," Jay claims, "The scales was lopsided, I'm just restoring order," speaking both of weighing cocaine and fighting gross injustice and restoring balance between black and white.

On the 2010 song "Shiny Suit Theory," made by rapper Jay Electronica, who is signed to Jay's Roc Nation record label, JAY-Z guest starred and flipped the tables on the therapeutic profession: instead of culturally incompetent shrinks treating black children, Jay puts psychiatry itself on the couch and gives it a rousing psychoanalytic read. Jay's narrator sets the scene with a therapist receiving a report about Jay that concludes he is delusional for believing that he, a boy from the hood, could share a cover with Warren Buffett, as Jay did on *Forbes* magazine in 2010.

> *In this manila envelope, the results of my insanity*
> *Quack said I crossed the line 'tween real life and*
>   *fantasy.*

Jay wasn't just giving psychiatry the bum's rush. He was also implicitly challenging the logic undergirding the American perversion of the *Geisteswissenschaften*, as

thinkers use philosophy, history, literary and cultural studies, and theology to justify the argument that black folk
are intellectually inferior, raving barbarians, or just crazy.
Clearly the psychiatrist represents white America and its attempts to convince black folk that we are loony for wanting to make it in America. Jay offers bracing bars that nod
to Rosa Parks and the divine redemption—better yet, the
divine conception—of hustling.

> *In the world of no justice and black ladies on the*
> > *back of buses*
> *I'm the immaculate conception of rappers-slash-*
> > *hustlers*
> *My God, it's so hard to conceive*
> *But it all falls perfect, I'm like autumn is to trees.*

The therapist "scribbled a prescription for some Prozac,
he said, 'Take that for your mustard,'" since "you gotta be
psychotic or mixing something potent with your vodka /
It takes a lot to shock us but you being so prosperous is
preposterous."

Wealth isn't just the aspirational goal of the desperately poor, but speaks to a will to overcome, to resist, to
rise from the back of the bus to hobnob with billionaires,
to even believe that one might become a billionaire one-
self someday. It is to combat racist forces that Jay asks
how a "nappy headed boy from out the projects / Be the
apple of America's obsession?" Jay's narrator doesn't just

fight back; he reverses the terms, underscores the racist rationalizations that deny black sanity and genius, and addresses the plague of overmedicating black kids. Certainly, overmedicating children is a national concern as we address the side effects of drugs that accompany the diagnosis of psychiatric conditions. But the racial fallout is heightened when black kids, who are already victims of an unjust, resource-starved, two-tiered educational system, are subject to medical intervention apart from careful, compassionate, culturally aware talk therapy.

Sometimes the delusions and rationalizations of race come from within blackness itself. The animated video for 2017's "Story of O.J.," directed by Mark Romanek and JAY-Z, features the character "Jaybo," a portmanteau of JAY-Z and Sambo and a withering visual and lyrical signification on JAY-Z himself. Casting himself, even in animated form, as a derogatory Sambo-like figure is a feat that Jay is able to pull off because he has spent a long career artistically reflecting on race. The life of JAY-Z glimpsed in song highlights the struggle and occasional conflict between his sense of once being black and poor and now being black and wealthy. If we argue that race is socially constructed, rather than built on genetics or biology, and that it is the broader social world that gives race meaning, then we might say that Jay's vision of blackness is *lyrically* constructed.

Back in 2003, when Jay was "Young, Gifted and Black," he likened himself to Public Enemy front man Chuck

D "standin' in the crosshairs." His crafty allusion to the PE logo is less about identifying with one of hip hop's most aggressively pro-black groups and more about underscoring how it felt to be black and vulnerable, forever caught in the crosshairs of the scope of an American gun. Racism is unfailingly aimed at young black folk, their dreams, their families, and their communities. As "Young, Gifted and Black" unfolds, Jay recounts the pain and the loss of living in the postindustrial malaise of inner-city America. Later in the song he returns to a familiar theme, namely, that he will not "shed a tear" for his losses, signaling the dehumanizing effects of concentrated poverty and the violence it begets.

If we fast forward from there to his 2006 duet with Nas, "Black Republican," a different take on blackness looms. Given the current state of race on the right, it is difficult to reconcile the lyrics of this catchy collaboration with the Grand Old Party as it stands now. Of course, in light of the Trumpian seizure of the moral assets of Republican ideology, it is rather easy to concede, in retrospect, that in brute comparative terms, the GOP may have stood for something qualitatively different than what they presently proclaim. It is not that the 2006 version of Republicanism flashed much empathy for black folk. After all, as we shall shortly see, Jay, among many others, assailed George W. Bush for his heartless abandonment of the black poor during Katrina. But at least the right paid lip service to a "compassionate conservatism" that is all but silenced in our present moment.

On the song, Jay and Nas claim to *feel* like black Republicans. The affect here is specific. For these two, after their epic battle, feeling like a black Republican is about making money—drug money or rap money, it doesn't matter. But the catch, and the sure signpost of their faithful blackness, is that they look back and give back to the hood. They "can't turn [their] back[s] on the hood / [we] got too much love for them." The hook is about giving back, giving black. Jay's verse on "Black Republican" is an urban hood tale about comrades in the rap and drug game who fall out and possibly reconcile as they realize all that is at stake. Of course, neither one is a Republican. The "Black Republican" title is simply a signifier for their desire to complicate conceptualizations of blackness itself.

Jaybo spends much of the video for "The Story of O.J.," arguably JAY-Z's best entry in his considerable body of audiovisual art, strolling the streets of New York City and, eventually, the world. "The Story of O.J." isn't a story about O.J. Simpson. The song uses an anecdote about O.J. distancing himself from his blackness as an occasion to advise and mentor Jay's audience about race, capitalism, and entrepreneurship. The visuals for "The Story of O.J." video, drawn in a black-and-white, faux early-twentieth-century minstrel aesthetic, present a litany of stereotypical images—blackface performances, minstrel dances, plantation workers, cotton fields, lynch mobs, and a factory that produces members of the Ku Klux Klan. In aggregate, and without paying attention to the words of the song, the images of "The Story of O.J." are patently offensive, especially to black folk. It is a lyrical wonder that JAY-Z's words, and the canny, wry expressions of the animated Jaybo, change the meanings of these images. The words of "The Story of O.J." reshape those images to deconstruct the history of racism.

But antiblackness isn't the only force that needs to be disassembled. The politics of black masculinity have to be laid bare as well, and Jay became a lightning rod for those offenses.

When *Everything Is Love*, by JAY-Z and Beyoncé (the Carters), appeared in June 2018 out of nowhere, by now their standard method of releasing new work, much of the world stopped for a moment. That pause was a collective holding of breath and a subsequent sigh of relief. The trilogy was complete. Fans of Beyoncé and her husband had no idea when *Lemonade* dropped in 2016 and changed the world that it was the opening salvo in arguably the greatest record-cycle trilogy ever produced in black music history. This had been perhaps the most thrilling appearance of Hegel in black culture since Martin Luther King's famous remix in the sixties of the nineteenth-century German philosopher's notions of a thesis, or statement of a position, its counterargument in an antithesis, and a final synthesis of the two.

First, there was on April 23, 2016, the thesis, *Lemonade*. This was Beyoncé's Arthur Janov–like primal scream of a record-as-therapy-session that unleashed mammoth waves of anger and grief, rocking the emotional ships of men the world over. It put us on notice that she, and by extension all women, would no longer tolerate the treacherous squandering of love, loyalty, faithfulness, and commitment. One of the most beautiful and powerful and adored women in the world commanded her artistic platform to amplify subversive melodies and defiant harmonies. And the culprit and cause of her pain was widely rumored to be her husband. He, like her, to keep the Hegelian theme going, was a world historical entertainment figure.

It felt voyeuristic to see any of this, like we had happened upon a heated quarrel about personal goings-on we had all gossiped about but had no confirmation for nor any business knowing. It felt uncomfortable to hold this knowledge. It felt obscene to see her suffering, and really, to see the suffering of millions of women the world over. It felt at once thrilling and tragic to witness these women take vicarious swings of the bat with Beyoncé as she smashed a car windshield in the longform video of the album.

This was unprecedented in black life. Sure, we see the carnage of black domestic disputes played out on "real housewives" franchises daily. But we cannot be certain that the presence of the television cameras hasn't overly filtered the reality through the prism of entertainment and the lens of racial reflex, of cultural expectation. This was for the cameras too, but it was far higher art. Yes, this was entertainment too, but ironically, in its bold artifice, in its constructed, deliberate aesthetic, in its carefully selected words and images, it was far more honest and revealing than any reality show. We hadn't seen this before, where the female member of a famous black couple told the truth about what it was that made their "us" a tenuous union.

It was as if Coretta Scott King had sat down to write "Letter from Birmingham Jail," except, in this case, it wasn't the white man's cage in which she found herself imprisoned. Instead it was her home, her heart, her head, her life, and what her life had turned into since loving and giving herself to the most remarkable man possible. But he had another side that she had dared not expose to the white world for fear they would use it against him to impugn his integrity and defeat his, and her, purpose. However, *Lemonade* is a different time. These are different circumstances. Jay and Bey aren't civil rights leaders, though they are justice warriors. There are different rules. Respectability politics aren't what they used to be, and the white world has been forced to make minor concessions to its hypocrisy of berating black folk for doing the same things that white folk do routinely.

And the power dynamic is totally different. The fracas

is public and the stakes are high. *Lemonade* threatened to become the greatest diss in music history. It is not a diss single, but several songs' worth of venom directed at the category *man*, not at any man in particular, at least not by name, so that its bitter genius is to signify without surrendering to a demand to be explicit. Interestingly enough, that is a demand made famous by the singer's former girl group Destiny's Child when they insisted that their cheating men "Say my name, say my name."

Jay could have chosen to ride things out since only assumption, or innuendo, or shady allegation and hushed-mouth eye-rolling could link him to his wife's acrimonious catharsis. He might have even been defiant in his denial and insisted that it was just music, just his wife's genius to tap into the feminist zeitgeist and its yen for female heterotopias, for comforting places to affirm their sublime difference. He might have taken the fifth and remained silent. Instead, on June 30, 2017, he released *4:44*, the antithesis not only to *Lemonade* but, truly, to the hem-hawing denials of men seeking to repatriate themselves to the monarchy of amnesia and the republic of avoidance.

Jay's self-critical rejoinders on *4:44* as he outed himself as the culprit are fairly unprecedented too. He clearly and straightforwardly admits his error, his sin, his failure. Of course, the implicit rebuff, often explicit protest, that underlay it all is *How dare he cheat on one of the most amazing and beautiful women on the face of the earth?* But that misses the point and undercuts Beyoncé's ability to symbolize "all" women, any woman, just as Jay's ability to embody all men doesn't ride on his difference but his similarity to "all" men.

We are forced to see the true source of the offense: the failure to honor the other in all we do, the failure to treat the other person as precious as ourselves, though, given the levels of self-hate and self-doubt that prevail, that standard may not ultimately hold either. It is, then, the failure to treat the other in a way that honors their worthiness to be respected as human beings regardless of beauty, standing, fame, or wealth. It is clear that Beyoncé takes a hit for the masses of women. But it's also clear that she challenges outmoded ideas about why the offense she endured was not something that all women could identify with.

Jay's response on *4:44*, and in interviews where he told his story, proves helpful because it models a masculine ethic of regard for the other as precious in herself, and that no matter the issues of self that rot one's relationship to the other, no excuses can possibly prevent an open acknowledgment of injury inflicted. There wasn't—and shouldn't have been—great detail given about the offense. That is truly the business of Jay and Bey. What is important for the public face of their collective persona is the willingness of Beyoncé to vent and Jay to voice the truth of what she vented; for him to see the righteousness of the path she chose to express her pain and suffering; and for him not to erode its intensity or its integrity with even the subtle qualifications in which dishonesty and denial hibernate. That is important for all relationships, but in this case, it is especially important for *black* relationships.

The Jay of *4:44* must be contrasted to the Jay of, say, "Big Pimpin'," in which he touts a callous, unenlightened black masculinity that views women as instruments of pleasure, scorn, or distraction. When men claim we are emotionless, as JAY-Z did in his October 2009 *O* magazine interview with Oprah, we rarely mean it literally. Men who supposedly have no feelings express joy in material gain and economic success. We have little trouble expressing anger at those who violate our territory or code of male ethics. Emotionlessness in most men turns out to be a euphemism, or rather, a misdiagnosis of sorts; it often refers to a very specific kind of emotional intelligence that many men code as feminine. Expressions of vulnerability, shame, and, as sad as it may sound, love must be erased or strictly contained. This is as much a failure of the broader culture's view of masculinity as it is the fault of any particular man. Thus Beyoncé takes on both generalized manhood and specifically unnamed masculinity. Unlike Jay in *4:44*, some men claim an emotionless profile as a badge of honor. When we think of toxic masculinity, its roots often trace back to a perilously narrow set of experiences deemed legitimate or desirable as we men negotiate the space we occupy on earth. The toxicity saturates our perspectives of manhood, taints and

damages us and our loved ones. It spills over in behaviors
that demean, degrade, domestically abuse, and, in extreme
cases, dispose of women without a sense of human compassion or the faintest trace of moral aptitude.

JAY-Z's confession of emotionlessness is a specific de-
tachment of feeling that he honestly engages. The journey
of JAY-Z from 2001's "Song Cry," about a man so emotionally constipated the tears couldn't flow, so the song
had to cry for him, to 2017's "4:44," illuminates the rapper's moral and masculine evolution. Jay's progress from
heartless lothario in "Big Pimpin'" to soulful empathizer
on *4:44* charts his own detox from the unfeeling JAY-Z
persona that appealed to his fans into a better, humbler,
and, yes, more emotional version of himself. Jay's narrator in "Big Pimpin'" is ruthless in his carnal desires and
erotic exploits. The narrator's Iceberg Slim pimping pedigree is proudly promoted.

> *You know I thug 'em, fuck 'em, love 'em, leave 'em*
> *'Cause I don't fuckin' need 'em*
> *Take 'em out the hood, keep 'em lookin' good*
> *But I don't fuckin' feed 'em*
> *First time they fuss I'm breezin'*
> *Talkin' about, "What's the reasons?"*
> *I'm a pimp in every sense of the word*

Contrast that to JAY-Z's unadorned apology in the
first line of "4:44," and his confession of the damage

wrought by infidelity, a perception that came home to him, literally, with the birth of his first daughter and later his twins:

> *Look, I apologize, often womanize*
> *Took for my child to be born, see through a woman's eyes*
> *Took for these natural twins to believe in miracles*
> *Took me too long for this song, I don't deserve you*

Jay's intentional turn away from poisonous patriarchy could help men who regard his past lyrical exploits as masculinist life manuals. Jay has proved in the past that his actions are consequential and paradigmatic. When Jay said "Change Clothes" in 2003, throwback jerseys—sports uniforms made to resemble team uniforms from the past—were discarded in lieu of "button-ups" and more traditional business attire. Yet a critical challenge remains. When Jay says to his life partner, "I apologize," when he confesses his faults, his infidelity, and reveals his sheer vulnerability in the face of his own failures as a husband and father, can we follow suit?

> *You matured faster than me, I wasn't ready*
> *So I apologize*
> *I seen the innocence leave your eyes*
> *I still mourn this death and*
> *I apologize for all the stillborns 'cause I wasn't present*

Your body wouldn't accept it
I apologize to all the women whom I toyed with
  your emotions
'Cause I was emotionless
And I apologize 'cause at your best you are love
And because I fall short of what I say I'm all about

To follow in Jay's path demands a death of ego that the artist expresses on the striking "Kill Jay Z," where he acknowledges responsibility to his daughter Blue and to the young folk who idolize him:

Kill Jay Z, they'll never love you . . .
And you know better, nigga, I know you do
But you gotta do better, boy, you owe it to Blue
Cry Jay Z, we know the pain is real
But you can't heal what you never reveal
What's up, Jay Z? You know you owe the truth
To all the youth that fell in love with Jay Z

Note, too, the semantic shift betokened in the change of the spelling of his name. He announced in the weeks before the debut of *4:44* that he was changing from Jay Z to JAY-Z, closing the gap once again in the two terms of his name, symbolically closing the gap in his own identity, perhaps, and emphasizing his new name, his new identity, as an all-in-caps truth that could be proudly trumpeted. The changing of names resonates in black life, especially, since black folk were often denied the ability to name themselves. Fresh from enslavement, there was a riot of naming in the first flush of freedom. Jay's real name, Shawn Carter, remains unchanged, but his public persona, his deliberately chosen linguistic vehicle of self-identification, matches his moral rebirth.

Following Jay along the path of healthy masculinity also invites the sort of systematic self-inventory he conducted while in therapy. To be sure, there are huge stigmas attached to psychotherapy or even general psychological counseling in many parts of the culture. It must mean you're crazy. It must mean you're weak. It must mean your faith isn't strong enough, that you haven't held Jesus's hand tightly enough. And, yes, there are cultural reasons that explain our particular skepticism as black folk too. Our mistreatment in the past, and too often in the present, by medical professionals doesn't just scare us away from the medical doctor, or the psychiatrist, but it too often makes us wary of any sort of therapeutic intervention. The belief that God might somehow be offended by therapy reeks of the most blatant form of disbelief in God imaginable. After all, if God created both the patient and the therapist, then God has it under control and knew in advance the kind of help we'd need. To reject it is to reject the help for which too many folks pray yet turn their backs on when it is sent their way.

Following JAY-Z will demand, too, the kind of aching masculine vulnerability that Jay showed in confessing his sins publicly. The world had already seen a glimpse of the box into which his painfully limiting masculinity had painted him when the recording of the elevator scene leaked in May 2014, nearly two years before *Lemonade*. There he is, in stark black and white, dressed to the nines, along with Beyoncé and her sister Solange, and their bodyguard Julius de Boer. As they get on the elevator, Solange first, she immediately begins to swing and kick at her brother-in-law, and Jay fends off her fists and feet, which are coming in a flurry, aimed at anywhere on his body. But he is too tall and he grabs her foot once and never strikes back, and she only connects three times, since de Boer is mostly holding her back. Beyoncé bears silent witness.

The scene might have spelled enormous trouble. There could have been days of public relations interventions and crisis management consultations. Instead, the trio released a single brief statement saying that the family had worked through their issues and that "Jay and Solange each assume their share of responsibility for what has occurred," and that each "acknowledge their role in this private matter that has played out in the public." What might have been an irrevocable embarrassment and stain on their reputations instead sparked growth, change, and some of the most affecting art and revealing music the couple has ever produced.

While black culture isn't the only culture to absorb

hardship and translate it into gain, the particular elements here suggest black traits of survival, black traditions of overcoming impossible odds—of taking lemons and making lemonade. That phrase was sampled from a video recording of a speech made by JAY-Z's grandmother Hattie White at her ninetieth birthday party in Clayton, Delaware, in April 2015. In a nice moral symmetry, JAY-Z's maternal line gave his wife the language to articulate both the bitterness of her predicament and the possibility of turning it sweet and satisfying. Jay and Bey's well-known habit of not speaking—not about the beginning of their relationship, not much about their wedding, not a great deal about their private affairs—served them well in cloaking this potential fiasco with the shroud of silence. But the silence clearly wasn't neutral, nor indifferent to the domestic trouble to which it pointed. Their lives and art are proof enough.

They turned a historic disadvantage of blackness, invisibility, in their favor, and made it a tool of their spiritual rebirth and moral awakening. As arguably the most visible couple on the globe—the Obamas are active, yet out of office, but Queen Bey and the King of New York are royalty forever—invisibility wasn't an obstacle but a lifesaver. It was quite a feat: the most visible black folk on earth retreated, in public view, while carrying on their lives, into a space they defined for themselves, on their terms, an existential black hole from which nothing, no information, no hints, no suggestions, no gossip, could escape. This method of playing everything close to the vest, of holding all at Bey, was not simply how they chose to release their recent music. It was also how they chose to release themselves from the images, views, beliefs, opinions, doubts, and commentary of the culture and outsiders, and their own fears and mistakes. This space allowed them to discover anew who they are in the infinite interiority of psychological solitude.

In pragmatic terms the trio won. Solange, a world-class pop artist and fashionista, came across as a woman who was ride-or-die for her beloved sister—and went on to release *A Seat at the Table* in 2016, a contemporary R&B and pop soul classic. Beyoncé, when she exited the elevator, looked, well, flawless. Jay later confessed on "Kill Jay Z" that he was dead wrong, "You egged Solange on / Knowin' all along, all you had to say you was wrong." In a September 7, 2017, Rap Radar podcast interview, Jay said of himself and Solange, "We had one disagreement ever. Before and after, we've been cool." He said that "[s]he's like my sister. I will protect her. That's my sister, not my sister-in-law. My sister. Period." Beyoncé talked about it through song without speaking about it otherwise. *Lemonade*, like the elevator video, is a recording of tumultuous reckoning. Beyoncé sang later on the "Flawless Remix": "But no, we escalating, up in this bitch, like elevators / Of course sometimes shit go down / When it's a billion dollars on an elevator."

Jay's mature and introspective masculinity on *4:44* opened the way for the Carters to make a record together. The pain of *Lemonade* and *4:44* will forever mark the records as locked in an epic lovers' quarrel. But the synthesis, *Everything Is Love*, which arrived on June 16, 2018, creates for listeners a third space for black lovers. It joins the first two entries in this mythic trilogy but stands alone in ways that the first two records cannot. It is, in so many ways, a testament to the endurance of black love and black relationships. Everything *is* love. On "Black Effect," Jay and Bey sing and rap in tandem about their love of blackness itself. It is still an astonishing and tragically rare feat for black artists to publicly love blackness in the face of the withering efforts to demean and diminish it.

Sometimes the daggers come from within. Jay has had to deal with the black self-hatred that would see him as ugly because of his features, especially his lips, perfectly formed African versions of labium superius oris and labium inferius oris that spit an entire universe of black beauty into existence. That rhetoric flows from an ocean of ideas inside a brain now shielded by a shock of glorious locs atop his head.

For these two artists to hold forth on this subject matter in this way helps to extend the very thing about which they sing and rap. Black love's black effect is given a black boost by two of the biggest and blackest stars on earth. No space is therefore foreign to them. No black body unlovable or undesirable. Jay and Bey's love is a contagious black love that loves all bodies and all black places.

That love, of course, includes same-sex and same-gender loving folk. When Jay shared with the world that his mother Gloria Carter is lesbian, he not only swam against deep tides of homophobia, but he rescued many souls drowning in self-hate or being pulled under by hatred and fear from other black folk. Several years ago, before the revelation of the queer identity of Gloria Carter, Duke professor Mark Anthony Neal, in his book *Looking for Leroy: Illegible Black Masculinities*, penned a chapter on JAY-Z, "My Passport Says Shawn," where he probed the "value of having the theoretical worlds of black feminist and queer theory . . . travel through the body of a highly visible and influential masculine icon of hip-hop." Neal proved prophetic since it is on JAY-Z's *4:44* album, in his words, in this particularly confessional and revealing body of work, that he helped his mother come out to the world.

Jay's and Beyoncé's love is at once personal and political, and, as they claim, "I'm good on any MLK Boulevard (I'm good)," which means they're good in any community where black people live. The naming and renaming of urban streets after black political and civil rights heroes has become the political pastime of a peculiarly American brand of incrementalism. Posthumous black heroes are often more palatable to the powers that be than living, thriving warriors who would push back at the limitations placed on black life. In death, Emmett Till's name claims a street in Chicago even though in life his humanity was utterly invisible to the white men who kidnapped, tortured, and murdered him. And so goes the eponymous reclaiming of countless urban boulevards in the name of Martin Luther King. I have never equivocated in my full-throated estimation of Dr. King as the greatest American who ever lived. He is that and more; and the fact that so many streets, avenues, and boulevards across urban America bear King's name is a stirring tribute to his transcendent status. But those tributes cannot obscure the irony of poverty that plagues many of the neighborhoods through which MLK Boulevards run. I am certainly not the first person to acknowledge this, but in most hoods, MLK Boulevards aren't the safest places to be. This fact makes Jay's and Bey's allusion to being "good" on any MLK Blvd the equivalent of saying that they are good in any hood. One cannot love black people without being able to love where they are from and commune with them where they are.

But Jay has also made sure to speak about other avenues to black survival that occurred long before streets got named after fallen icons. The specter of slavery haunts the African American mind and shadows a society that too often refuses to acknowledge its complicity in this nation's most grievous offense. On "Oceans," which,

like "Made in America," features a hook by R&B singer
Frank Ocean, Jay takes stock of the nearly incomprehensible loss of black life in the transatlantic slave trade. That
unspeakable horror marked bodies as chattel and shipped
them to North American ports of call. Slavers were able to
do evil deeds in the name of the marketplace and religion.
Thus, it became clear that the slavers' theology permitted
them to reconcile the beef between God and mammon
in promoting a racist gospel. Tragically, their approach
echoes today in white evangelical heretics who try to trump
Obama because they deem him Beelzebub while heralding
Trump as a political savior.

Right off the bat, Jay situates the blood of the black
enslaved who died in the oceans with the ravages of another form of disaster capitalism when he observes, "The
oil spill that BP ain't clean up." Jay proceeds to connect
European imperial ventures to American discovery, challenging the ballyhooed patron saint Christopher Colum-
bus revered in our collective imaginations and enshrined
in our history books. He offers, instead, the prospect of
reverence for the dead but not forgotten Brooklyn MC
Biggie Smalls. "I'm anti-*Santa Maria* / Only Christopher
we acknowledge is Wallace." He follows it with a figurative association that seals his insurrectionist impulse. "I
don't even like Washingtons in my pocket," he insists.

What might he mean here? Not liking such small
denomination bills; not liking the history of a president
who enslaved black folk; not wanting a white face in his

pocket. Hence his next line, "Black card go hard when I'm shopping," symbolizes a level of elite status not easily attained even by those who would slight Jay today. Once again it suggests wealth as a means to oppose racism. It suggests, too, the superiority of a product created by a black man, Kenneth Chenault, who was at the helm of American Express when the black card was introduced. (It is not hard to imagine the symbolic value to black folk, and the broader culture, of the most exclusive charge card on the market being a black one.) Perhaps Jay simply didn't want the filth and lucre associated at times with the U.S. Capitol to soil his pockets. Jay finishes the verse contrasting slave ships with his yacht, but this time his boat "docked in front of Hermès picking cotton," as his fate as the offspring of enslaved ancestors permits their bejeweled progeny (he refers to his Jesus piece, jewelry showing the face of the Savior and made famous in hip hop circles) to practice a bit of compensatory economic justice.

After all, when he says that he will "lay [put] on my Jesus," he not only adorns his neck with jewelry, but he conjures images of captured Africans forced to lie atop each other in slave ships, especially *Jesus of Lubeck*, the first slave ship to darken the West. Jay brags that, emboldened by his ancestral energy, "I crash through glass ceilings, I break through closed doors," in proxy of the women and men in the past whose flesh was enslaved, and black folk now whose lives are hampered by obstacles. All of this makes sense as Ocean sings, "Because this water drown my family, this water mixed my blood / This water tells my story, this water knows it all." Those who lost their lives and whose blood spilled in the waters tell a story of a people stolen, bound, and shipped, and later castrated, raped, and murdered, whether lynched from trees or thrown into the Mississippi River. This is what it has meant to voyage inside the hull of the American experiment.

Jay has consistently taken on American ideals, American myths, and American illusions, whether sitting in on an instant classic by rapper Meek Mill, "What's Free," to up the ante and point out American hypocrisy ("In the land of the free, where the blacks enslaved / Three-fifths of a man, I believe's the phrase"), or letting loose on "A Ballad for the Fallen Soldier," one of JAY-Z's most sophisticated critiques of American patriotism and American law enforcement. The song's lyrics cling to an extended analogy between "street" soldiers and conventional soldiers in the throes of American empire. Jay compares the state of the nation after the 9/11 terrorist attacks and the ongoing siege of black America, using a slant rhyme to offer his slant on things:

> *Bin Laden been happening in Manhattan*
> *Crack was anthrax back then, back when*
> *Police was Al 'Qaeda to black men.*

JAY-Z uses an experience Americans are familiar with as a bridge to an experience that is largely foreign to them—

the vulnerability and disposability of black life in what feels like a police state.

The song is a phenomenology of existential dread, a glimpse into the torturous state of affairs for black folk—a completely arbitrary form of relentless assault that leaves them exposed and defenseless. Every time a black body is senselessly beaten by a baton, bloodied by a fist, pummeled while prostrate with hands secured behind the back, hunted and harmed, or mercilessly shot on purpose with no good reason, black life is in terror. And then to have it all happen time and again until it is ingrained in black minds to leave our blackness behind. That, by the way, is impossible, though we attempt to do so by swallowing ourselves inside of our fear. But that never works either, because we are, invariably, shot in cold blood like wild animals, indeed far worse than wild animals. This is the sense of terror that JAY-Z seeks to express. This is the coerced helplessness in the face of a gory Neapolitan dessert consumed by the streets: vanilla cops, chocolate bodies, strawberry blood spilled from black limbs.

If "Bin Laden been happening," then this joyless ballad is for those who have fallen prey to destruction in their illegal activities in the underground economy *and* for those who have fallen victim to police brutality whether they are guilty or not. Herein lies the terror: in the end it makes little difference in how we are seen or treated. And for those who deem it hyperbole to compare the assault on black life to terrorist attacks, the failure to see the parallel only increases the distance between black and white, only increases the suffering.

On so many other songs, Jay tells truths: about police brutality, about stalled criminal justice, about the value of generational wealth, about white supremacy, about the need for black love. These truths might be lost to the audiences that buy his records or download his music, if he didn't entice, seduce, brag, exhort, and party. Conscious rap's appeal, the allure of "wokeness," is undeniable, especially in a culture combating recrudescent bigotry and the vicious toll of white supremacy. But Jay knows that if the music doesn't move your behind it has little chance to stimulate your brain. Many, as we have seen, have taken that to mean he isn't smart or sophisticated, when he is both. They've used his approach to dismiss his political urgency and racial relevance, when, clearly, he's got both in spades.

On "Minority Report," JAY-Z dramatically effects sotto voce in a somber tone. "My peoples was poor before the Hurricane came," he hauntingly chants about Katrina's fury. The solidarity of his opening line stings because human solidarity was painfully absent in the aftermath of the storm. The survivors were seen as "refugees" in their own nation. The racial division was clear: white folk were "searching" for scarce resources while black folk were "looting." Some black folk paid the ultimate price for this racist distinction, even after surviving one of the greatest disasters the nation had ever experienced. JAY-Z's "Minority Report" brought home to me how the black poor had long ago been abandoned by our society and cruelly assaulted by black elites like Bill Cosby. The comedian-cum-social-critic tagged the black poor as fatally promiscuous, nearly allergic to education and good speech; he said they saddled their kids with weird names and were eager to blame the white man for their ills.

The concept of a "minority report" is straightforward enough. It is an opinion that officially dissents from the majority in a group. In this instance it has racial significance. Jay's view of Katrina dissents from that of the white majority and the government. The idea of a minority report resonates strongly in black culture, where views on race in particular often run counter to the mainstream. One might reasonably argue that some of hip hop's best lyrics should be included alongside the many such reports from black culture over the centuries. These reports might include, for example, Sojourner Truth's "Ain't I a Woman," Ida B. Wells's *Red Record*, Maya Angelou's *I Know Why the Caged Bird Sings*, and Angela Davis's *If They Come in the Morning: Voices of Resistance*. They are all minority reports, all dissenting from what passes as racial common sense.

To be sure, the word "minority" clashes with the idea of a global network of people of color. "Minority" is often a euphemism for black folk that at once names and yet eviscerates black experience. The term, useful as it may be in some instances, centers white history as a norm and surrenders linguistic territory to white dominance, perhaps even white supremacy. Jay's "Minority Report" pushes back against all of this. While others let the black poor float in the deadly waters, and still others drowned them in stigma, shame, and a river of lies, Jay lays claim to New Orleans residents as *his* people, a life-affirming assertion in the midst of death. But he does more than talk; he makes a monetary contribution to their welfare. Still, he is introspective, yielding a powerful gesture of self-criticism as he takes measure of his failure to respond as courageously and as responsibly as he might have.

> *Sure I ponied up a mil' but I didn't give my time*
> *So in reality I didn't give a dime*
> *Or a damn, I just put my monies in the hands*
> *Of the same people that left my people stranded*
> *Nothin' but a bandit, left them folks abandoned.*

My peoples, Jay says, and again, my people. Simple phrases with profound meaning. He affirms a relationship of racial intimacy driven by empathy and trust, a trust he felt he had broken. Ne-Yo sings the brokenness in a searing retort on the hook: "Seems like we don't even care."

"Minority Report" also subtly alludes to the 2002 Tom Cruise film of the same name. In the movie, based on a Philip K. Dick short story, the prophetic abilities of a group of enslaved psychics are exploited to serve the surveillance state. Their predictive talent is harnessed for the "PreCrime" unit, which snags would-be offenders before they commit crimes. The film grapples with the perils of determinism in a fictional dystopic future. But for black folk this is hardly a matter of science fiction. Sadly, we exist in a world where "PreCrime" apprehensions are routine, even predictable. Our criminal justice system may as well be operated by psychics given the arbitrary nature of justice for black people and the troubling racial inequities that poison the system itself.

JAY-Z learned his lesson from the incidents described in "Minority Report" and grew more sophisticated in his response to the politics of race. In fact, if Jay can be said to have established a political hub, if there is a centripetal force that gathers his various efforts in a tightening gyre, it is in reforming the criminal justice system. JAY-Z has had personal dealings with the American justice system and can testify to how financial resources can deflect the "minority report" effects of a racist system. He says as much when he quips on "99 Problems" that it's "Half a mil' for bail 'cause I'm African." In 2018, after penning a *Time* magazine op-ed the previous Father's Day criticizing the bail industry and pretrial incarceration, JAY-Z and his business partners made a first-round capital investment of $3 million in Promise, a bail reformation and decarceration start-up company. Bail reform hardly speaks to the horrid practice of locking folk up—who have yet to be convicted of crimes—for months, sometimes years.

But JAY-Z could hardly say that to the family of Kalief Browder.

JAY-Z, as Shawn Carter, executive produced *Time: The Kalief Browder Story*, a six-episode docuseries that appeared on Spike TV in 2017. The series painstakingly documents the crushing psychological and economic effects of the bail system on one family. Kalief Browder was sixteen years old when he was arrested in 2010 for a robbery he claimed he didn't commit, and then spent more than a thousand days in jail on New York City's Rikers Island awaiting a trial that never occurred. During his jail time he was assaulted by an officer and savagely beaten by a menacing throng of inmates. He spent two years in solitary confinement and attempted suicide several times, tragically achieving his goal in 2015, two years after he was released from jail, when he could no longer battle his demons. The series indicts the system itself. But neither the film, nor, for that matter, Ava Duvernay's brilliant documentary *13th*, nor the Promise bail reform effort, nor hip hop lyrics are sufficient to end the ruthless monied bail system or eradicate its racial inequities. But each, in connection with other grassroots and long-term efforts, forms a powerful witness on behalf of millions of black lives gobbled up by a punishing criminal justice system.

Perhaps Jay's advanced understanding of the flaws in the criminal justice system began to take shape earlier in his career when he was not merely an artist but also at the helm of a record label, recruiting talent for his roster. Philadelphia proved to be especially fertile artistic territory. There Jay found a full slate of lyrically gifted hood soldiers shaped in the cauldrons of Philadelphia's remarkable underground hip hop scene. Oschino Vasquez, Omillio Sparks, Freeway, the Young Gunz (a duo comprised of Young Chris and Neef Buck), and Beanie Sigel all hail from the city of brotherly love. Each of these artists had varying degrees of success on Dame Dash, Kareem "Biggs" Burke, and JAY-Z's Roc-A-Fella Records between the late 1990s and the first decade of the new millennium. Beanie Sigel was the most talented of the bunch, although Freeway nearly matched him in lyrical skills and popularity. But "Beans" had great difficulty separating his rap career from his life in the underground economies of his native haunts. These challenges provoked Jay to admonish Beanie Sigel about his perilous choices on record. Still, as early as 2000, JAY-Z was becoming aware of how the criminal justice system aggressively operates in Philadelphia.

Beanie Sigel flashed entrepreneurial savvy and helped to form both a clothing line and a rap group (consisting of Sigel, Young Gunz, Oschino Vasquez, Omillio Sparks, Freeway, and Peedi Crakk) named State Property. The clothing line, a subsidiary of Rocawear, made headlines for its seamless sartorial synthesis of prison life and the streets. It is hard to miss the clothing's symbolic gesture in its name: the justice system captures, contains, and controls black and brown bodies as state property. In retrospect, JAY-Z and hip hop, indeed the culture at large, had far different views than they do now about criminal justice reform. There were certainly artists who scorned police brutality and tried to lyrically check the system for its anti-black biases. HBO's *The Wire*, a hip hop fan favorite, debuted in 2002 and grappled with many of these issues. But the impetus to criminal justice reform had not taken hold in social and political circles the way it has today, especially since the publication of Michelle Alexander's *The New Jim Crow* in 2010.

Not surprisingly, perhaps, things didn't turn out well for State Property. Their stage name proved prophetic. Beanie Sigel was arrested in 2004, and the group, clothing line, and JAY-Z's deep investment in Philadelphia hip hop all began to fall apart. But the specter of an aggressive criminal justice system that relies on the fear and ignorance of the citizens it is supposed to protect and serve continued to haunt Jay. Like any great artist he worked out his issues through his work. One of the most powerful products of his artistic encounter with the criminal justice system is the song and video for 2004's "99 Problems."

The first verse of the song puts the media in its crosshairs. Radio, magazines, and advertisers profited greatly from JAY-Z's brilliantly successful career, but he assails critics who reduce his music to "Money, Cash, Hoes." In the second verse, Jay amps up the tension in a lyrical anecdote from 1994 about being followed and pulled over for "doing 55 in a 54." Verse two is a mini-clinic on the legal limits of traffic stops and searches. When asked by the police officer if he knows why he was stopped, Jay's narrator replies: "'Cause I'm young and I'm black and my hat's real low." The third verse narrates yet another run-in with the criminal justice system. This time, Jay's narrator is "Back through the system . . . again," and saddled with a huge bail because he is black.

While Jay's indictment of the criminal justice system's bias against blacks is skillfully interwoven in his lyrics, it may not be as apparent—even though JAY-Z's hustling persona is always front and center—that the narrator in verse two is driving with a stash of drugs. "[M]y trunk is raw," he claims in that verse's first line. And the narrator of verse three is clearly engaged in retributive violence. In each tale, Jay's narrators are guilty of some of the very crimes that the criminal justice system often unfairly accuses black folk of committing. But for black folk, the bias against guilty and innocent alike remains the same.

Too often people of color are victims of a vicious one-two punch: On the one hand, if they are innocent of a crime, they are told that the reason they are suspected is because black people commit more crimes than white folk. This, of course, fails to account for how such bias is a self-fulfilling justice system prophecy. Because of broader suspicions about black humanity and character, black folk are taken into the criminal justice system more often than white folk, not because the white folk are innocent of offenses but because they're not suspected of them in the first place.

On the other hand, if black folk are guilty, those of us interested in true justice are made to feel immoral and unjust for pointing out that they receive far harsher penalties than similar white offenders.

That is why criminal justice reform must include sentencing reform. Since most of the crimes black people commit, or are accused of committing, are nonviolent, it makes sense to release from incarceration nonviolent substance abusers, low-level drug dealers, and those charged with nonviolent possession of marijuana in every state that has legalized the controlled substance for medicinal and recreational purposes.

Yet we cannot simply reform the criminal justice system; we must fundamentally transform it. We must re-imagine how we treat those who are guilty—even those who are guilty of violent crimes. We could experience true redemption if we were to rethink the morality of incarceration. In a very subtle way, the guilt of JAY-Z's narrators in "99 Problems" permits a more nuanced critique than if his characters were innocent. But his approach is also an invitation to reflect on the injustice of a system that incarcerates more folk than any other in the world.

Jay is doing his part, which involves more than rapping: he penned poignant *New York Times* opinion pieces on the failed war on drugs and on the cruel fate of younger rapper Meek Mill, who, for the last several years, has been in and out of jail because of what appear to be arbitrary and draconian actions of the state due to parole violations. Jay argued in November 2017 as an elder statesman of rap and exposed the dysfunction of a system of justice he knows all too well.

> *What's happening to Meek Mill is just one example of how our criminal justice system entraps and harasses hundreds of thousands of black people every day. I saw this up close when I was growing up in Brooklyn during the 1970s and 1980s. Instead of a second chance, probation ends up being a land mine, with a random misstep bringing consequences greater than the crime.*

For each way that Meek Mill is singled out for reproach by the state—he and JAY-Z are friends after all—Jay takes the issue and connects it to the broader injustices of the system. Jay uses Meek's situation to illumine policies and inequities that "hundreds of thousands of black people every day" face. And most do it without the aid, as Meek received, of noisy, visible protests, without the interventions of a cultural icon, and without a successful rap career to fall back on. James Baldwin popularized telling the truth as widely and eloquently as possible, and Jay bears witness in this way.

To that end, JAY-Z, seeing the need to reform and

enact policy, joined with Meek Mill, Philadelphia 76ers partner Michael Rubin, New England Patriots partner Robert Kraft, philanthropist (and wife of Brooklyn Nets partner Joseph Tsai) Clara Wu Tsai, and Vista Equity Partners founder and CEO Robert F. Smith, among others, to create the REFORM Alliance, with CNN host Van Jones as CEO. The alliance's stated mission, according to a press release, is to advance "criminal justice reform and [eliminate] outdated laws that perpetuate injustice, starting with probation and parole." As he has done throughout his career, Jay continues to move from the artistic to the political.

Jay's political awareness also bubbles up in his references to black leaders such as Rosa Parks, Malcolm X, Coretta Scott King, Jesse Jackson, Betty Shabazz, and especially Al Sharpton and Martin Luther King, Jr. To be sure, the mentions are more honorable than primary, more instrumental than substantive. For Jay, King is an emblem of the future through the fulfillment of his dream: "Let's talk about the future / We have just seen the dream as predicted by Martin Luther," he says on "What We Talkin' About," from 2009, referring to the link between King and Obama. On 2001's "The Ruler's Back," Jay proclaims that "I'm representin' for the seat where Rosa Parks sat / Where Malcolm X was shot, where Martin Luther was popped."

Note that Jay doesn't represent these figures per se; he would never presume such a stirring feat of racial ambassadorship. But he does represent the places of their struggle and death in a kind of architecture of prophetic personification. He sees their greatness despite their humiliations and (some of their) tragic deaths. He sees them as symbols of overcoming and victory, but not before they meet the bus seat, ballroom floor, or motel balcony of their destinies. Jay represents the spots and occasions of their transformations not as tokens of the hate that arrested them or the evil that snuffed them, but as the sites of their transition from earthly icons to heavenly saints. He is, by means of his words, a symbolic facilitator, interpreting these figures' meanings and readjusting our understanding of their relevance to our moment. Although he was a service laborer in the underground economy, Jay, like them, faced the site of his potential ruin and reached a spot of transfiguration as a cultural icon. The crack corner joins the seat, the floor, and the balcony as the place where rebirth through symbolic or literal death occurs. Perhaps Jay's words, and hip hop's words more broadly, can give new meaning to King at the site of the fallen leader's humiliation and symbolic death as recent news claims to reveal more of his flaws.

Before that, however, Jay's jibing and jousting with Sharpton is revealing. It may seem to be a throwaway line, but JAY-Z's words on the second verse of 2017's

"Family Feud" have deeper meaning and more history than one might hear upon first listening.

Al Sharpton in the mirror takin' selfies.

Jay is referring to Reverend Al Sharpton's Instagram post on June 18, 2017, wishing his followers a Happy Father's Day as he snapped a selfie while heading to a workout at dawn. The post went viral. Sharpton, usually nattily clad in expensive designer suits, was sheathed in navy blue workout gear that included oversized trunks and white Nike sports socks pasted between his calves and sneakers.

Sharpton took the light jab in good humor. In several media appearances, he professed his love for Jay and ribbed him for being jealous of his routine. He admonished the almost fifty-year-old rapper to step it up, saying that he'd repay him by slipping his name in a couple of his sermons, and suggested that he was flattered to be name-checked yet again. Jay had cited Sharpton fifteen years earlier on his 2002 song "Diamond Is Forever," which addressed a real-life fracas that Jay had in 2002 with tenants of a luxury apartment building who feared that his notoriety would distress their quiet halls. According to *Billboard* magazine in February 2002, some of the tenants posted messages in the lobby cautioning residents against Jay's "criminal record and lifestyle of knives, guns and violence," concluding that if the rapper were allowed to move into the building he would "place us in danger." Jay vented on record, countering with a threat of his own to bring in Sharpton and Jesse Jackson to protest the injustice.

> *Old lady, don't blow my high*
> *'Specially if you don't know my life, don't make me*
>   *bring*
> *Sharpton in it 'cause I'm dark-skinn-ed or*
> *Dude with the 'fro and the Rainbow Coalition.*

A mere five years later, Jay got in a spat with Sharpton about his response to radio host Don Imus's attack on black players of the Rutgers women's basketball team as "nappy-headed hoes." In light of Imus's crude remarks, critics claimed that hip hop was even more at fault for demonizing black women in misogynistic lyrics. Sharpton, who led the charge against Imus, said that he "would not stop until we make it clear that no one should denigrate women," and that "ho and the b-word are words that are wrong from anybody's lips." The minister took to the streets in protest against three major record labels and their support of rap that disparaged black women. Critics contended that by drawing an equivalence between hip hop entertainers and Imus, Sharpton was conflating artistic expression and radio commentary, and that he failed to see the difference between white racist assault and undeniably sexist black art.

> *I missed the part when it stopped bein' 'bout Imus*
> *What do my lyrics got to do with this shit?*

Jay made this tart retort to Sharpton and other critics in 2007 on "Ignorant Shit," cleverly using a homophone to link Imus and "I miss."

Some claimed that if Imus were a rapper, instead of being forced off the air he'd have a hit record. It was a sly way to escape responsibility for his racist and sexist rant. Of course, both sexism in rap and white racism should be addressed. But some thought it was wrong to let Imus enjoy a form of white privilege and set the agenda: his self-pitying complaints about unfair treatment in comparison to that of rappers sparked social protest against misogyny in hip hop. Jay framed the conflict on 2007's "Say Hello" as a tug of war between artistic self-expression and systemic social injustice. Jay drew a line between an empowering leadership that fights structural inequality and a moralizing one that tries to curtail black male speech.

> *And if Al Sharpton is speaking for me*
> *Somebody give him the word and tell him I don't*
>   *approve*
> *Tell him I remove the curses*
> *If you tell me our schools gon' be perfect*
> *When the Jena Six don't exist*
> *Tell him that's when I'll stop saying bitch,*
>   *BEEEITCH!*

Of course, JAY-Z and Sharpton both had a point: it is perfectly legitimate to combat racial injustice while resisting the sexism and misogyny that corrupt hip hop culture.

Civil rights leaders and other prominent figures have been easy prey in hip hop as rappers unfavorably compare present activists to past luminaries. Too often they are unaware that many of the same charges they bring against Sharpton or Jackson were made against Martin Luther King, Jr., in his day—that he was an ambulance chaser, that he sought the spotlight, that he was hopelessly vain, that he was a reckless interloper. West Coast rapper The Game and Nas capture this stance on their moving 2008 homage to Martin Luther King, "Letter to the King." Nas's verse laments the betrayal of King by some of his contemporaries who are still alive. "Some of your homies phonies, I should've said it when I see them / Them sleazy bastards, some greedy pastors, jerks / Should never be allowed at Ebenezer Baptist Church in Atlanta."

The Game conjectures that if King were alive and marching today, the rapper could readily predict which leaders would support him and which would fall away. "I know Obama would, but would Hillary take part?" (In fact, when he ran for president the first time, Obama famously skipped the gathering that marked the fortieth anniversary of King's death at the National Civil Rights Museum in Memphis, built on the spot where King was slain. Clinton attended and spoke. So did Republican presidential candidate John McCain. After he left office,

Obama missed the museum's fiftieth anniversary gathering in honor of King's death.)

The Game made a poignant query on the song's final verse that recycled a wild and unfounded rumor of Jackson's complicity in King's murder. "I wonder why Jesse Jackson ain't catch him before his body dropped / Would he give me the answer? Probably not." The negative comparison of Jackson to King mirrors Lil Wayne's spoken coda to his 2008 song "Dontgetit," where, over a sample of Nina Simone's "Don't Let Me Be Misunderstood," Wayne reflects on the war on drugs and child molestation and offers a nasty, bitter tirade on Al Sharpton. "Uhh, Mr. Al Sharpton, here's why I don't respect you, and nobody like you. Mmh, see, you're the type that gets off on gettin' on other people." He takes Sharpton to task for allegedly judging folk before he gets to know them, in particular Wayne himself. "You see, you are no MLK, you are no Jesse Jackson. You are nobody, to me. You're just another Don King . . . with a perm. Just a little more political." Sharpton shot back on the website *The Fix* that his crusade against degrading women in rap lyrics had led some rappers to despise him, but that a Gallup poll revealed that he had "a 50% approval rate among African Americans," making it unnecessary to "dignify a response to one rap artist who doesn't even say anything substantive." Five years later, the publishing arm of Cash Money Records, home to Lil Wayne, released Sharpton's memoir *The Rejected Stone*.

The argument in hip hop circles and beyond that Sharpton doesn't measure up to Jackson, and that neither of them measures up to King, reflects a deep chasm between memory and history, between perception and truth. Both ignorance and amnesia spur us to romanticize icons like King while heaping scorn on leaders today. If we knew more about past leaders, their flaws and frailties, as well as their courage and valor, we might appreciate current leaders more. The willingness to take a hard look at black icons in religion, politics, and entertainment would serve us well. Today we grapple with figures who test our racial loyalty, our moral limits, and our ability to call a spade a spade. Jay follows up his line about Sharpton on "Family Feud" with another equally provocative bar. "How is him or Pill Cosby s'posed to help me?" Simply by means of a satiric misspelling of Cosby's first name, Jay signifies a complex web of interrelated arguments about celebrity, black protectionism, and the hypocrisies that stalk black life.

My own work over the last quarter century analyzing the lives of talented but troubled black men, from King to Bill Cosby to R. Kelly, has permitted me to reflect on the stakes and perils of telling the truth about black men in the presence of white America.

As we have seen, a selfie taken by Reverend Sharpton, the leading contemporary civil rights leader of his generation, pointed to a deeper, longer history of engagement between the two men than that single photo suggested, spotlighting a bigger story than what we might otherwise see. The same is true for an iconic 1958 photograph of the young Martin Luther King, Jr., that offers us more than meets our eyes. The history behind the photo lurks beneath the image we see and invites us to think about how we view gifted but flawed black men. The photograph of King is striking. He is decked in a natty tan suit, a shiny gold watch bright on his wrist and a snazzy broad-banded snap-brim fedora snug on his head. A cop is twisting King's right arm behind his back and pinning his shoulder down to the police station booking desk as another cop stands guard. For one of the rare times in King's life, this arrest had nothing to do with civil rights. King was charged with loitering at the courthouse as he sought to enter the preliminary hearing of a case involving his closest friend and fellow civil rights leader, Reverend Ralph Abernathy. The case involving Abernathy had nothing to do with the movement. Abernathy had been attacked in his church and chased down the street by a hatchet- and gun-wielding black schoolteacher named Edward Davis, who claimed that the Alabama pastor had been having sex with his wife, Vivian Davis, since she was fifteen years old.

The subsequent Davis trial caused a scandal in Montgomery's black community. Salacious details leaked of oral sex between Abernathy and Vivian in a relative's home. There were claims that Edward Davis had been recruited by hostile whites to bring down Abernathy and taint the movement. Davis was quickly acquitted and divorced his wife as Vivian fled town. Abernathy found solace in a black community that protected its leader, insisting that it believed him and assuring him that all would soon return to normal. It did. Abernathy's plight reminds us that prominent black men accused of wrong, legally or morally, face a dual reality: a white world that often harms and sits in harsh judgment of black life, and a black world that provides balm for our wounds and nurture for our grievances, and sometimes, forgiveness, or even cover, for our sins. It is often difficult for black folk to grapple with the flaws of a famous figure because the context of their misstep, or downfall, is colored by the belief that the white world doesn't play fair.

Several years after Abernathy's ordeal King confided to a fellow leader that he had known of some of Abernathy's infidelities because he had taken part in some of them himself. King was a far guiltier adulterer than Abernathy. The FBI pummeled King with its voyeuristic surveillance of his sex life. The ugly venture was presided over by J. Edgar Hoover, whose obsessions with King highlight his own sexual hypocrisy, damning King's sexual misadventures while enjoying quite a few of his own in his airtight closet as a gay, cross-dressing destructive figure. But none of Hoover's proclivities forced him from office or subjected him to the kind of immoral Bureau scrutiny that King endured.

"They are out to break me," King declared on an FBI recording, and black folk agreed, whether "they" were the FBI specifically or white society generally. The white folk who found King's consensual sexual behavior repugnant worried little about the same behavior among white leaders. To be sure, what set King apart from his white male compatriots was a brutal racial hierarchy that morally taxed black life while giving white people exemption. Still, both white and black society shared in toxic masculinity. King may have battled white supremacy with full force, but he gleefully waved the white flag to bristling chauvinism. He believed his talented wife, Coretta, should stay at home with the kids. He took full advantage of the erotic possibilities that endlessly swirled around him. And he once joined a raucous chorus of male staff laughter at the recounting of a party that boasted a prostitute and the near sexual throttling of a seventeen-year-old Southern Christian Leadership Conference secretary.

I received a great deal of black criticism when I published my first book on King nearly twenty years ago. I discussed his plagiarism and adultery because I felt it my duty to reckon with his genius and flaws. King, to me, is the greatest American this nation has seen. He levied the moral authority of black protest against the scornful force of white resistance to make democracy sing in full-throated vibrancy. I also knew that black folk had complained that white folk could only see the moral beauty of their heroes, and not their faults. One of the most grievous faults of some white heroes is that they blocked black growth and diminished our achievements. Still, their faults were heedlessly ignored while their virtues were wildly overplayed.

I thought King deserved better, that he could withstand the truth, and that his singular strengths meant that we should look history squarely in the eye and take note of his overwhelming greatness and his undermining failures. I did so not because I was perfect or blameless but because I witnessed how black folk damned youth culture for the same issues that plagued King: a fascination with sex, a delight in words sometimes not his own, an obsession with death. In a sense black folk repeated the sin of white folk: they loved their heroes but overlooked the flawed appeal of their own children. If King could shake loose from his mortal peril to embrace the future with determined hopefulness, so could they. But they couldn't move forward looking at King as an icon of perfection while viewing their children and the culture they produced as pathological. Telling the truth about King was a way to insist on the hidden truth and obscured value of our kids.

The urge to protect King and other black icons is understandable, but it is an impulse that is often misplaced and easily exploited. Moreover, not all black figures are equally deserving of such protection. When Bill Cosby began to berate poor black folk in public, he was widely hailed in black America for telling difficult truths. I saw it differently. Bill Cosby was part of an out-of-touch black elite—what I call an "Afristocracy"—that pilloried the black poor, the "ghettocracy," for their moral failings and cultural deviance. Cosby in an infamous 2004 speech in Washington, D.C., lambasted black folks' unique names ("names like Shaniqua, Taliqua, and Muhammad and all that crap, and all of 'em are in jail"), their use of black English ("I can't even talk the way these people talk. 'Why you ain't, where you is go'"), and mating habits ("Pretty soon you're going to have to have DNA cards so you can tell who you're making love to . . . might be your grandmother").

I got huge blowback in black circles in 2005 for my criticism of Cosby, with people claiming that I was trying to pull a black man down. Many contended that I had no right to criticize a man who had done so much for black America, particularly his philanthropy in support of black colleges. I found it ironic that many black folk defended Cosby against my criticism while praising his vicious criticism of the black masses. I wrote at some length about the allegations of Andrea Constand and Lachele Covington against Cosby and faced stern rebuke in many barbershops and church sanctuaries. (One prominent New York City church refused to display my sermon topic criticizing Cosby on its outside billboard.)

While Cosby lashed out against black youth for their sexual and social perversions, he was allegedly engaged in an astonishing and extended rampage of sexual assault that sharply contrasted with his comedic genius and humanitarian endeavors. Cosby exploited black paranoia about white efforts to bring down prominent black men. The racist impulse to check black power and progress surely exacerbated the tendency among black folk to embrace conspiracy theories about wide-ranging and orchestrated attempts to harm black life. While he rebuffed the black poor for conveniently resorting to race to explain their troubles, Cosby willfully leaned on race to gin up the eruption of black protectionism for himself. That protectionist sentiment has failed to die down even as Cosby now sits in a prison cell.

Similarly, black protectionism seems to have allowed R. Kelly to cast a spell on black America for decades. (Early on in his career, JAY-Z collaborated with Kelly for two albums.) The 2019 *Surviving R. Kelly* documentary—produced by longtime JAY-Z collaborator dream hampton—has finally brought to a fever pitch the effort to hold the enormously troubled superstar accountable for his alleged sexual abuse of mostly teenage black girls. It was long rumored that in 1994 twenty-seven-year-old Kelly married R&B star Aaliyah when she was fifteen, a marriage that was quickly annulled. Kelly has since been charged with child pornography, including making an infamous sex tape with a thirteen-year-old girl, and sexual abuse and other predatory behavior; most recently he has been hit with twenty-one charges of sex abuse in Illinois, prostitution and solicitation charges in Minnesota, and federal charges of sex trafficking. The lure of Kelly's musical genius kept black folk willfully ignorant and awkwardly silent for decades. I wrote about Kelly extensively in my book *Mercy, Mercy Me*, and interviewed him in his Chicago compound in the wee hours one October morning in 2003. I have always believed that Kelly should suffer the consequences of his actions as well as seek therapy to confront his demons. But it would be too easy to hold Kelly accountable—as he unquestionably should be—and let other black men who exploit and prey on teenage girls and young women off the hook. The problem of black girls and women being ignored, taken for granted, or abused is an ongoing plague we have barely addressed.

Muting R. Kelly, at least until he comes to grips with the horror he has caused, is one necessary thing. But picking and choosing who to mute is trickier than it may appear on the surface. Marvin Gaye, at the direction of his barren wife, impregnated her sixteen-year-old niece. Later, he had a public relationship with a high school girl, and he got her pregnant four months after they met. Should we mute him too? Miles Davis was brutally abusive to his wives, and Michael Jackson is alleged to have sexually abused children. Should they be muted too?

The monstrous and brazen nature of Kelly's offense may seal his fate. Torn for most of his career between the flesh and the spirit, Kelly has bluntly begged people in his music to intercede with God on his behalf: "Instead of you all throwing them stones at me, somebody pray for me," he pleads on "I Wish." Yet Kelly is unwilling to meet the Almighty or believers halfway. Absent an acknowledgment of his wrongdoing, a confession of his sin, Kelly is unlikely to receive either the grace of God or the forgiveness of the people. Kelly told me in an interview more than fifteen years ago that, "When I put out stuff like 'I Believe I Can Fly,' the real true God warriors are gonna start praying for me. And intervening for me. Because they know I got a monster at me."

Believing that God will somehow overlook one's failures and flaws because one has offered the world a gift is hardly unique to R. Kelly or the millions who, because of his genius, dismiss his predatory pedophilia or his sexual abuse. Abernathy found consolation in the arms of black believers who were willing to forgive him or look the other way because of his valor in the face of evil. He later made an odd confession—not of his own sin, but that of his fallen comrade Martin Luther King, Jr. When King lived it made sense for Abernathy to speak for him as his second in command and a chief interpreter of his social and moral aims. But after King's death, presuming to do so, especially on such an intimate matter as sex, was more troubling. Abernathy contended that the night before King died, King, after delivering his last and arguably greatest speech, had sex with two women at different points of the night and in the early morning physically fought a third female "friend." It was tragic to many folk that Abernathy had talked about King's secrets and sins, something King had refused to do to his best friend.

In his own way, King confessed his own sins, warning his congregation not to think of him as perfect when he declared in a sermon, "You don't need to go out saying Martin Luther King, Jr. is a saint." (In 1968 he confessed to his wife that he'd had a mistress since 1963 who meant the most to him of all the women he saw outside his marriage, a married woman who lived in Los Angeles. But the timing was disastrous. Coretta was recovering from a hysterectomy, and King was bitterly scolded by Abernathy's wife, Juanita, who told him he should take his guilt to God or the psychiatrist.) Of course, Abernathy's confession of King's sins might have been read as Abernathy finally breaking ranks with the poisonous patriarchy that clouds black culture. And yet, for that to be true, Abernathy would have had to tell on himself as well, to give account of his own flaws. And about those flaws he remained deadly silent. It is a hypocrisy that too many of us know all too well.

In the spring of 2019, noted King biographer David Garrow said in the conservative British publication *Standpoint* that he'd got hold of newly released FBI documents that take fresh aim at King's sex life. These are based on memos of alleged transcripts and audio recordings that are sealed in the National Archives until 2027. Garrow had written in his King biography *Bearing the Cross* about what he termed King's "compulsive sexual athleticism," figuring that the civil rights leader had ten to twelve girlfriends over four to five years. Now it seems that King had from forty to forty-five paramours over that time period. There are also claims that King engaged prostitutes; fathered a child outside of his marriage; and participated in orgies, including one with a female gospel legend. Most damning of all—though far less reliable—he had, according to a note scribbled on the FBI file, "looked on, laughed and offered advice" as a ministerial colleague raped one of his parishioners. On another occasion, King is said to have told a reluctant participant in an "unnatural" sex act that it would "help your soul."

These claims have been challenged by historians, who have good reason to doubt their veracity. The FBI, after all, was hardly a neutral observer of King and meant explicitly to destroy him. But I proceed here as I always have, with an eye to figuring out the most damning thing that might be true about King, and then working back from that premise. Thus, should extremely compromising and damaging revelations be found to be true about him when the files are unsealed, we will have already wrestled with the most egregious and harmful claims.

If the most serious charges are true, that King witnessed and found humor in rape, that he coaxed a woman to agree to troubling sex, it is tragic and shows just how deeply entrenched King was in the toxic masculinity and rape culture that have poisoned so many men for so long. Garrow concludes in his *Standpoint* article that "a profoundly painful historical reckoning and reconsideration inescapably awaits."

Yet many books on King, especially works by Garrow, Taylor Branch, and me, have grappled at length with King's sexual appetites and proclivities. What the trove of FBI documents does show is the rabid racism of the FBI and their pornographic preoccupation with King's phallus. There is an erotics of white supremacy that Garrow seems to miss, a psychological resentment of black virility that fuels the insanity of surveillance. The FBI bugged King's hotels and home to determine if he was hanging out with communists, but the surveillance quickly became a referendum on his bedroom behavior.

The files may give us a greater sense of King's behavior, but will likely also reveal our government's willingness to destroy and obscenely invade the life of a private citizen who posed no threat to the nation. What King challenged was white supremacy; what he opposed was the fierce bias against blackness; what he wanted was justice for all folk. And for that desire he was hounded, harassed, harmed, and then shot and killed. He lived daily with the threat of death. He had uncontrollable hiccups brought on by fear. The government that was supposed to shield him from harm made him more vulnerable to attack. Perhaps King drank and sexed so much because he realized just how disposable his black body was in a culture that hated his skin and despised his breathing. This is no excuse at all for laughing at a woman being raped. But to divorce King's sex life, and the toxic choices he made, and the great harm he may have caused from a logic and culture that made those choices seem reasonable or acceptable is to settle for symptoms not sources, for effects and not causes. Rape and race culture alike have polluted the nation's moral mainstream.

King taught us to forgive our way to freedom, to love our way to justice. The same should hold for him. He knew he was far from perfect, and yet, even in his imperfections, he forged ahead to make real change. When we think of King in the late fifties and sixties, heavily drinking, deeply depressed, intensely grappling with the unseemly ubiquity of death so that we wouldn't have to die, we can, and should, forgive him. This is not the same, by the way, as pretending those sins—those great flaws and profound offenses—don't exist, or overlooking the harm that he may have caused. But he is not here to ask for forgiveness himself, in part because he died for us, a death that freed many of us to learn about ourselves so that we could embrace the freedom to criticize him in good conscience and just deliberation.

King's face in the famous photo was stoic as the cop manhandled him and pinned him down. Too often our faces have looked the same as we have attempted to pin down our just reactions to the tragedies that have come our way. Like King, we must steel ourselves to face down the forces of social and personal injustice as we come to grips with our own complicity in the suffering we see.

JAY-Z has had to face his own demons too, but in a far more public way than the fallen leader he often cites in his lyrics. In a way, JAY-Z's courage in confronting his sins and imperfections suggests a way forward for our understanding of King too. The vulnerable rapper of "4:44" paves the way posthumously for a hobbled King to reclaim his humanity and dignity despite his grave mistakes.

> *Look, I apologize, often womanize*
> *. . .*
> *I seen the innocence leave your eyes*
> *I still mourn this death and*
> *. . .*
> *I apologize 'cause at your best you are love*
> *And because I fall short of what I say I'm all about*
> *Your eyes leave with the soul that your body once*
> *　　housed*
> *And you stare blankly into space*
> *Thinkin' of all the time, you wasted it on all this*
> *　　basic shit*
> *So I apologize*

Jay is teaching in a lot bigger classroom than I'll ever teach in . . . For a young person growing up he's the guy to learn from.

WARREN BUFFETT

Highlighting the social stereotypes superimposed on African Americans in hip hop, JAY-Z states that despite his success in corporate America, as both artist and executive, that he is a "nigga." Using this term of endearment used between many African American men and women in African American culture as well as hip hop, JAY-Z aligns himself with the continued struggles of many black subjects who follow him aspiring to rise above their social conditions and to obtain the wealth and success that he models in his career.

NICOLE HODGES PERSLEY

"What's Better Than One Billionaire?"

In June 2019 *Forbes* magazine announced that JAY-Z was a billionaire, the first hip hop artist ever to attain that status. The news was widely applauded in black circles because Jay is only the fifth black billionaire in the land, joining Robert F. Smith, Oprah Winfrey, Michael Jordan, and Dave Steward. The pride black folk take in Jay has more to do with his origin story than with mere wealth, although Jay has become a vocal evangelist for developing generational wealth in black communities. It is Jay's story of uplift from the gutter to the heights of global acclaim and vast riches that makes his success irresistible. The fact that a former street hustler and crack dealer has cracked the top echelon of wealthiest citizens is simply miraculous.

Of course, there are those in black life who will contend that Jay's success is little more than a black face on capitalism, the vicious consequences of which have often ruined black life. That is true. But it is also true that Jay's ascent is a token of the irrepressible spirit of black folk in the face of impossible odds. Having been a poor black boy without resources or help from privileged black circles, he is truly free to celebrate his success as a nod to the folk from the bottom who gave him hope and inspiration, including those folk with whom he hustled in the street. If anything, Jay's success is an argument against respectability politics. It is eloquent witness against assailing poor blacks who have been abandoned by most of society.

JAY-Z's status is driven not only by his entrepreneurial genius—unlike many wealthy folks, he made it through his own hard and inventive work—but by his uncrushable desire to use what God gave him to lift himself and those who look like him. It is not that becoming a billionaire vindicates Jay's hustling, his poetry, or his politics; it is that it offers him an even more visible platform to amplify his voice to speak about black love, black struggle, black death, black success, black wealth, black overcoming, and black thriving. Instead of shutting up, the richer he gets the louder he speaks; instead of receding, the wealthier he becomes the more visibly he gets involved in speaking for the vulnerable.

In the end, it is not his wealth that has made JAY-Z but his hustling ethic, his poetic invention, his political savvy, and his business acumen. It may be that Diddy soon, and perhaps Dr. Dre someday, will join JAY-Z as black billionaires who hail from hip hop. Until then, JAY-Z will continue to work to inspire others to catch his vision and do what he does. He said it best.

> *What's better than one billionaire? Two (two)*
> *'Specially if they're from the same hue as you*
> *Y'all stop me when I stop tellin' the truth.*

No, the proliferation of black billionaires can't save us. No, they can't compensate for the justice due to the masses of black folk. (Although it is encouraging that Jay has become a brand strategist for the cannabis company Caliva, advocating for increased representation and participation of formerly incarcerated folk who are blocked in large numbers from the weed business.) No, they are no proxy for reparations. No, they are no replacement for the systemic overhaul of institutions that harm us. No, they are no substitute for challenging over-incarceration, the criminalization of the black poor, the dehumanization of the black masses, police brutality, systematic disenfranchisement, and every other problem we face.

Neither can becoming a black billionaire spare one from cultural blowback. In August 2019, Jay's company Roc Nation announced a partnership with the NFL to advise the league on live music and entertainment and projects of social justice. Jay was dubbed a hypocrite and a sellout for pivoting from his principled defense of former NFL quarterback Colin Kaepernick to doing business with the very league whose teams were accused of colluding to banish him for kneeling during the national anthem to protest racial injustice. Jay had even worn Colin's jersey while performing on *Saturday Night Live* and advised other artists to boycott the Super Bowl halftime show. In an interview announcing the partnership, when asked about Kaepernick, Jay said, "I think we've moved past kneeling. I think it's time for action."

The ensuing verbal lashing of the legendary rapper reminded me of Malcolm X's attacks in 1963 on Martin Luther King, Jr. Malcolm, who advocated armed self-defense of black folk in the face of white supremacists, flayed King, who preached nonviolent resistance to social injustice. "The white man pays Rev. Martin Luther King, subsidizes Rev. Martin Luther King, so that Rev. Martin Luther King can continue to teach the Negroes to be defenseless," Malcolm charged. King was a "modern Uncle Tom." Malcolm also dubbed King "the best weapon that the white man . . . has ever gotten."

Kaepernick and JAY-Z are not the modern-day equivalents of Malcolm and King, but those pairs reflect an eternal tension—between the outside agitators who apply pressure and the inside activators who patrol the halls of power, bringing knowledge and wisdom—in civil rights and black freedom movements. King worked with the Eisenhower, Johnson, and Kennedy administrations to better conditions for black folk and to craft civil rights legislation. Jay, for his part, as I have discussed, has advocated for social justice in his music and beyond the stage for more than two decades. The choice between Kaep and Jay, between Malcolm and King, is a false one. We need all of them, and it is far too early to judge what Jay will make of this opportunity with the NFL.

Jay's action fits into a tradition of social protest, forged by Jesse Jackson and Al Sharpton, that extends King's work: You protest a company—say a shoemaker or an auto dealership—for its unjust practices; you force those involved to acknowledge the error of their ways; you negotiate for better terms of engagement; you interact with the folk you once protested against in the effort to make progress. This reflected a shift in civil rights strategy from street protests to suite participation. Jackson leveraged the threat of boycotts and the rhetoric of persuasion to get more blacks placed on corporate boards, compel banks and major companies to direct more business to minority-owned contractors, and help integrate more black and other minority folk into the nation's economic power base.

It is true that the NFL did not explicitly acknowledge wrongdoing in Kaepernick's case, though the league did settle his lawsuit in February 2019, suggesting that it recognized his claim of collusion as a real legal threat. Jay cannot make a team hire Kaepernick, although perhaps Roc Nation could have refused a contract until Kaepernick got a job, which would have been a just outcome. But it is also true that social justice doesn't hinge exclusively on Kaepernick's employment. It would be a good thing for Kaep to rejoin the league, but his return wouldn't solve the oppression and injustice that his kneeling sought to highlight. Other efforts at both protest and policy were always called for and are still needed. Moreover, the fact that many team owners support an openly racist president demands an attempt to grapple with them. And it may be a sign of progress that those same owners got into business with a rapper who calls President Trump a "superbug." Jay's noisy opposition to white nationalism is just as important as how his partnership may provide the league cover.

Jay did not write off protest when he said we are "past kneeling." He simply cast Kaepernick as a runner in a relay race rather than a boxer fighting alone in the ring. The Players Coalition, for instance, was founded in 2017 by Philadelphia Eagles strong safety Malcolm Jenkins and former receiver Anquan Boldin to tie kneeling to serious and thoughtful action. It promotes social justice advocacy, education, and distribution of resources on the local, state, and federal levels. When it accepted nearly $90 million from the NFL to advance its agenda in November 2017, then 49ers safety Eric Reid, Kaepernick's courageous compatriot, called the thoughtful Jenkins a "sellout" and a "neocolonialist." But consider the coalition's efforts so far. As part of the $89 million that the players got the NFL to commit over a seven-year period, $8.5 million was allocated in 2018. The Players Coalition also does advocacy work with—and gave $2 million in grants to—the Advancement Project, the Center for

Policing Equity, the National Juvenile Defender Center, the Justice Collaborative, Year Up, and Communities In Schools. After Trump canceled a White House invitation to celebrate the Eagles' 2018 Super Bowl victory, Jenkins skipped a traditional news conference and drew attention with a series of signs clarifying that player protests weren't about the national anthem but about social inequality.

When white institutions and individuals ask for help (the request may or may not begin sincerely, but may evolve with more contact and better understanding), it is a good thing to supply it. Malcolm X once famously rebuffed a young white student who tracked him down in New York to ask what she could do to help the cause. His response took her aback: "Nothing." It makes for great theater and dramatic storytelling, but it was the wrong answer.

Things are never ideal, and systems of white oppression co-opt us all: teachers, advocates, athletes, organizers. I don't spare myself. I have spent nearly five decades—in speeches, books, and college courses—advocating for social justice. Yet I teach at Georgetown University, a school that sold 272 enslaved souls, including children, to bankroll its future. This is how the world works: All of us have blood on our hands and dirt beneath our nails, and we can scarcely afford to reject every institution we encounter as irretrievably tainted. The charge of being a sellout, and the instinct to "cancel" people indicted in this way, often comes full circle. (Malcolm was later deemed a traitor to his cause and murdered by members of his own group.) The language of betrayal cannot provide lasting moral satisfaction. Instead, as JAY-Z has amply provided, we need a vocabulary of moral accountability and social responsibility that is nuanced and capacious, giving us air to breathe and room to grow.

Jay's deal with the NFL represents a valid and potentially viable attempt to raise awareness of injustice to black folk, and to inspire the league to embrace just action for the black masses. Alongside scolding, resisting, protesting, and cajoling, there is a need for strategy, planning, listening, learning, and testing the application of principles embodied by people like Kaepernick.

The history of social justice advocacy is rich: King, Rosa Parks, the NAACP, the Student Nonviolent Coordinating Committee, the Freedom Riders, the Congress of Racial Equality, and a host of other organizations occasionally bickered over methods and messaging and strategy. But they were all motivated by grand ideals and good ends. Malcolm X, once he freed himself from his earlier narrow views, concluded that "Dr. King wants the same thing I want—freedom!" So does Colin Kaepernick. So does JAY-Z. And so should we all.

What JAY-Z symbolizes is a sweet spot in the culture's evolution as we continue to lay claim to what we are owed, forging ahead with a vision given to us by our ancestors.

ANNOTATED DISCOGRAPHY*

REASONABLE DOUBT, Roc-A-Fella/Priority Records, 1996.

After the buzz surrounding JAY-Z's 1995 independent single "In My Lifetime," the rap world was ready to hear what he could produce over an entire album. Released independently on June 25, 1996, _Reasonable Doubt_ did not disappoint. JAY-Z's first studio album was dripping with golden era hip hop production provided by DJ Premier, Irv Gotti, Ski, and DJ Clark Kent. _Reasonable Doubt_ has several standout tracks, including "Dead Presidents," "Can't Knock the Hustle," and "Ain't No Nigga"—a breakout single introducing the world to femcee (female emcee) Foxy Brown. _Reasonable Doubt_ offers a glimpse into JAY-Z's life as a drug dealer/hustler turned rap art-

---

* With two exceptions, this discography provides citation information and annotations for each of JAY-Z's formally released studio albums. One exception, _Jay-Z Unplugged_, is his only live studio album. The second exception is _Watch the Throne_, Jay's collaborative effort with fellow rapper Kanye West.

ist. Other notable songs from the album include The Notorious B.I.G. collaborative effort "Brooklyn's Finest," "D'Evils," "Politics as Usual," and "Can I Live."

The album teems with every poetic device imaginable. That includes allusion, on "Can't Knock the Hustle," when Jay's narrator nods to Psalm 23:5 and proclaims "My cup runneth over with hundreds"; double entendres and puns, such as "Stop screaming, you know the demon said it's best to die/And even if Jehovah witness, bet he'll never testify" on "D'Evils." The luxurious metaphors flow on "Cashmere Thoughts": "Uhh, I talk jewels and spit diamonds: all cherry/Like a hymen, when I'm rhyming with remarkable timing/Caviar and silk dreams, my voice is linen/Spitting venom up in the minds of young women/Mink thoughts to think thoughts type similar/Might you remember, my shit is cold like December"; and the similes pour smoothly like the best wine on "Dead Presidents II," where his narrator brags, "By the ounce, dough accumulates like snow/We don't just shine, we illuminate the whole show."

In 2002, six years after its release, *Reasonable Doubt* was finally certified platinum. With several subsequent documentaries explaining the process and importance of *Reasonable Doubt*, the album is now considered a seminal contribution to the art form and stands the test of time like few (hip hop) albums can.

IN MY LIFETIME, VOL. 1, Roc-A-Fella/Def Jam
Records, 1997.

Released on November 4, 1997, *In My Lifetime, Vol. 1* sold over 138,000 copies in its first week. With radio-friendly singles such as "Who You Wit II," "(Always Be My) Sunshine," featuring R&B impresario Babyface and Foxy Brown, and "The City Is Mine," featuring singer-songwriter-producer Teddy Riley's second notable group (after Guy), Blackstreet, JAY-Z's second effort came off without a hint of the sophomore slump. The record offered commercial appeal while not undercutting Jay's street credibility. Although the singles did not necessarily strike a chord with fans, almost every other song on the album stands out. Tracks like "I Know What Girls Like," featuring Puff Daddy and Lil' Kim, and "Face Off," featuring Sauce Money, were confirmed dance club hits.

However, the anchors of *In My Lifetime, Vol. 1* are the songs that extended the essence of the hustler-turned-rapper experience. The DJ Premier–produced tracks "Intro/A Million and One Questions/Rhyme No More" (and its slather of metonym and synecdoche, "I got mouths to feed 'til they put flowers on me/And kiss my cold cheek/Chicks crying like I was Cochise/Tombstone read, 'He was holdin' no leaks'") and "Friend or Foe '98" are boom-bap classics. Then too, the penetrating "Rap Game/Crack Game" and the searing "Where I'm From" further cement JAY-Z's reputation as a brilliant poet and wordsmith. "Streets Is Watching" finds JAY-Z flowing effortlessly over Ski Beatz's paranoid production. This is the only track from the album that Jay was able to share with Biggie before his murder in March 1997. Interestingly, "Streets" shares something in common with a track, "Gimme the Loot," from Biggie's first album, *Ready to Die*: it appears in censored form even on the album's explicit version. "Streets" uses a sample from the 1975 song "I Got The," by the British musician Labi Siffre, who refused to clear the sample unless the profanity was purged. (Eminem used the sample on his breakthrough track "My Name Is," curses and all.) Jay's lyrics summoned a cinematic experience so vivid that he and his label partners shot and produced a film of the same name. *Streets Is Watching* (the film) was released on May 12, 1998. *In My Lifetime, Vol. 1* debuted at #3 on the *Billboard* charts and was certified platinum.

VOL. 2 . . . HARD KNOCK LIFE, Roc-A-Fella/ Def Jam Records, 1998.

With the commercial success of *In My Lifetime, Vol. 1*, JAY-Z established a name for himself as a viable hip hop artist. By 1998 he was well on his way to cultivating a loyal and devoted fan base. The film *Streets Is Watching* is interwoven with an extended collection of music videos, featuring several notable songs from *Reasonable Doubt* and *In My Lifetime, Vol. 1*. The accompanying soundtrack included the single "It's Alright," featuring Jay's once-constant partner from the hood, Memphis Bleek ("Bleek could be one hit away his whole career/ As long as I'm alive he's a millionaire," Jay pledged on the remix to Kanye West's "Diamonds from Sierra Leone"), which would go on to be a hit single and was featured as a bonus track on JAY-Z's third album, *Vol. 2 . . . Hard Knock Life*. Released on September 29, 1998, *Vol. 2 . . . Hard Knock Life* debuted at #1 on the *Billboard* 200. It sold over 350,000 copies in its first week and won the Grammy award for Best Rap Album at the 41st Grammy Awards. The album featured a number of singles, including the Timbaland-produced tracks "Can I Get A . . . ," featuring onetime rap heavyweight Ja Rule and JAY-Z female protégée Amil, and "Nigga What, Nigga Who (Originator '99)," featuring Jaz-O and Amil. The album also featured the Swizz Beatz–produced "Money, Cash, Hoes," a collaborative effort with rising rap star DMX. The title track of the album, "Hard Knock Life (Ghetto Anthem)," produced by DJ Mark the 45 King, samples "It's a Hard-Knock Life" from the Broadway musical *Annie*. Critics and aficionados point to the massive success of the "Hard Knock Life" single as a pivotal point in JAY-Z's rise to global popularity.

VOL. 3 . . . LIFE AND TIMES OF S. CARTER,
Roc-A-Fella/Def Jam Records, 1999.

As the '90s came to an end, JAY-Z aptly and eloquently claimed that "the new millennium is upon us." So too was the JAY-Z brand. With JAY-Z firmly established as a hip hop icon, his fourth album, *Vol. 3 . . . Life and Times of S. Carter*, represents a branching out of sorts, both musically and in terms of marketing and promotions. Released on December 28, 1999, selling 462,000 copies in its first week, and debuting at #1 on the *Billboard* 200, the album coincided with a slew of featured singles on other projects, including "Girl's Best Friend" from the soundtrack for the 1999 film *Blue Streak* and "Jigga My Nigga" from the Ruff Ryders Entertainment compilation album *Ryde or Die Vol. 1*. (It was also included on *Vol. 3* as a hidden track.) Both of these songs are bonus tracks on *Vol. 3 . . . Life and Times of S. Carter*. Producers on the album include signature JAY-Z collaborators DJ Premier, Swizz Beatz, and Timbaland, among others. Like *Vol. 2 . . . Hard Knock Life*, this album continues JAY-Z's commercial reach with expansive success. The singles include the Rockwilder-produced track "Do It Again (Put Ya Hands Up)," featuring Amil and Beanie Sigel, the Chauncey Mahan / Swizz Beatz–produced track "Things That U Do," featuring sensational songbird Mariah Carey, and perhaps the biggest single of JAY-Z's career to this point, the Timbaland-produced track "Big Pimpin'," featuring the renowned Port Arthur, Texas, duo UGK. There is a noticeable shift in mood and tone on *Vol. 3 . . . Life and Times of S. Carter*. While JAY-Z appears to be experimenting sonically and diversifying his subject matter, the product has a uniquely refined quality that sets a high musical bar for the twenty-first-century boom in commercial hip hop. The album was certified triple platinum in February 2001.

ROC DYNASTY: ROC LA FAMILIA, Roc-A-Fella/ Def Jam Records, 2000.

By the time JAY-Z was ready to release what was intended—and turned out—to be the Roc-A-Fella Records compilation album, the label's premier artists had also enjoyed a measure of success. Memphis Bleek's *Coming of Age*, Beanie Sigel's *The Truth*, and Amil's *A.M.I.L. (All Money Is Legal)*, along with JAY-Z's massive commercial success, gave rise to what would be known in hip hop circles as "the dynasty." They would all be featured prominently on JAY-Z's *The Dynasty: Roc La Familia*, released on October 31, 2000. The album also showcased new productions from up-and-comers The Neptunes, Just Blaze, and Kanye West. The singles included the hugely successful "I Just Wanna Love U (Give It 2 Me)," produced by The Neptunes; "Change the Game," featuring Beanie Sigel and Memphis Bleek; and "Guilty Until Proven Innocent," featuring R. Kelly, a precursor to JAY-Z and R.

Kelly's two future hip hop/R&B collaborative album efforts. The sonic textures of *The Dynasty: Roc La Familia* represented a new era of sample-heavy, soul-based sound for JAY-Z that would carry over into his work in the 2000s. *The Dynasty: Roc La Familia* debuted at #1 on November 18 on the *Billboard* 200 and sold 557,789 copies in its first week.

THE BLUEPRINT, Roc-A-Fella/Def Jam Records, 2001.

On September 11, 2001, the United States of America experienced a terrorist attack of nearly incomprehensible magnitude that would alter the nation forever. That same unforgettable day, JAY-Z released his sixth album, *The Blueprint*. (That is also the date when I released my book *Holler If You Hear Me: Searching for Tupac Shakur* and began my book tour, in Boston, the city the terrorists flew from to commit their atrocities. Before my plans changed, I had been scheduled to appear at my first book event on 9/11 at the World Trade Center.) Though the album sold over 427,000 copies in its opening week, 9/11's tragedy overshadowed what would later be widely hailed as one of the greatest hip hop albums ever produced. *The Blueprint* prominently features the soul-sampled productions of Kanye West and Just Blaze. The singles include "Izzo (H.O.V.A.)"; "Girls, Girls, Girls," which features additional vocals by hip hop legends Q-Tip, Slick Rick, and Biz Markie; and "Song Cry." Other notable songs include the Kanye West–produced "Takeover," which would advance one of hip hop's most memorable feuds between JAY-Z and Nas. "Renegade," featuring Eminem, who produced the track (the only guest appearance by another rapper on the project), juxtaposes two of the most popular hip hop artists and lyricists of the 2000s in competition with each other. And "Heart of the City (Ain't No Love)" is perhaps the song that jump-started the career of Kanye West as a highly sought after hip hop producer. There is a maturity to the sound and the content of *The Blueprint* that shifts JAY-Z's career arc from enormous commercial appeal to universal artistic acclaim. While *The Blueprint* did not win any music awards, it is considered by many critics and fans to be one of the greatest albums of any genre of all time. In 2019 the Library of Congress selected it for preservation in the National Recording Registry for its cultural and aesthetic significance.

MTV UNPLUGGED, Roc-A-Fella/Def Jam Records, 2001.

Not long after JAY-Z released *The Blueprint*, he followed up with a set recorded live at MTV Studios in New York City. On December 18, 2001, *JAY-Z: MTV Unplugged* was released. Many of the songs are live versions of notable tracks from *The Blueprint*, along with singles from earlier in JAY-Z's career, including "Nigga What, Nigga Who," which was censored to "Jigga What, Jigga Who," "Big Pimpin'," "Can I Get A . . . ," "Hard Knock Life," and others. Legendary drummer, author, and audiophile Questlove and The Roots (featuring Black Thought, one of the greatest emcees in hip hop history) performed as the band for the live set. The Roots are considered one of the premier bands in hip hop, indeed in American music, as proved by their gig as the house band for *The Tonight Show with Jimmy Fallon* since 2009. And their ability to create musical synergy with JAY-Z is what made this one of the most important live albums in hip hop. Mary J. Blige and Pharrell Williams were also live guest features, with Blige on "Can't Knock the Hustle/Family Affair" and with Williams on "I Just Wanna Love You (Give It 2 Me)." An interesting symbolic gesture that JAY-Z would reference later in his career is the photo of Argentine revolutionary Che Guevara on the shirt he wore for the set.

THE BLUEPRINT²: THE GIFT & THE CURSE, Roc-A-Fella/ Def Jam Records, 2002.

Similar to the concepts of *Vol. 3 . . . Life and Times of S. Carter* and *The Dynasty: Roc La Familia*, *The Blueprint²: The Gift & The Curse* reflects an expanded roster and the extended reach of JAY-Z and Roc-A-Fella Records. Released as a double album on November 12, 2002, *The Blueprint²: The Gift & The Curse* debuted on November 30, 2001, at #1 on the *Billboard* 200 and shipped 545,000 units in its first week. The album featured heavy production from The Neptunes, Kanye West, and Just

Blaze, but it also featured veteran producers such as Timbaland, Dr. Dre, No I.D., and Heavy D. The album also featured a host of guest appearances, including Beyoncé, Dr. Dre, Rakim, Faith Evans, Lenny Kravitz, and newly signed Roc-A-Fella Records artists M.O.P., Kanye West, Freeway, and Young Guns. The first album is *The Gift*, and the second album is *The Curse*. *The Gift* supplies us with the singles "Hovi Baby"; "'03 Bonnie & Clyde," featuring Beyoncé on a JAY-Z song for the first time; and "Excuse Me Miss." In general, *The Gift* is an album filled with commercially viable, radio-friendly songs, thematically symbolizing JAY-Z's ascent beyond the first installment of the JAY-Z brand and into new pop celebrity status. *The Curse*, in contrast, provides a darker sound and no singles. The standout songs include the epic tale of "Meet the Parents" and the poignant ghetto escapist fantasy of "Some How Some Way," featuring iconic Houston rapper Scarface and Philly's Beanie Sigel. *The Curse* reflects a deeper, more conscious JAY-Z persona, one that was more in line with what he offered on *The Blueprint*.

THE BLACK ALBUM, Roc-A-Fella/Def Jam Records, 2003.

Released on November 14, 2003, *The Black Album* was JAY-Z's eighth full-length studio project, and it was billed as his last in light of his impending retirement. *The Black Album* did not end up signaling JAY-Z's permanent retirement, but it is considered by critics and hip hop aficionados to be one of the two or three best records in his long career. Outstanding cuts include "99 Problems," "Dirt Off Your Shoulder," and "Change Clothes," among many others. *The Black Album* is nearly 4X platinum. "99 Problems," produced by Rick Rubin, was made into a powerful music video where "JAY-Z" is killed in the concluding shot. The artist was not subtle about his retirement plans or his decision to put the "JAY-Z" artistic image to rest. Nor would this be the last time he proposed to metaphorically snuff his constructed artistic persona.

The producers on the album include 9th Wonder, Rick Rubin, Just Blaze, The Neptunes, and Timbaland. The general themes of *The Black Album* were consistent with JAY-Z's mature persona and commensurate with his status as an aging but still-dominant "king" of rap music and hip hop culture. Tracks like "What More Can I Say," "Moment of Clarity," and "Threat" (with a hilarious feature from Cedric the Entertainer) are designed to both excavate and celebrate JAY-Z's triumphant style and his extraordinary accomplishments. *The Black Album* is intended as a farewell, but JAY-Z hardly sounded disengaged with the art form, and his skills hadn't diminished so as to justify his exit from the game. In fact, some of this material (e.g., "Public Service Announcement") is among JAY-Z's most inspired work. *The Black Album*, ranked 349 on Rolling Stone's 2012 list of 500 greatest albums (*Blueprint* was initially ranked 464 in 2003, but in the revised list in 2012 it was bumped up to 252), was nominated for a Grammy for Best Rap Album in 2004 but lost to Kanye West's *The College Dropout*.

KINGDOM COME, Roc-A-Fella/Def Jam Records, 2006.

Released on November 21, 2006, *Kingdom Come* was not among JAY-Z's most critically acclaimed studio albums, and the artist himself has dissed this album as his worst. Both he and the critics are plain wrong. *Kingdom Come* is JAY-Z's "comeback" album, even though few critics or fans believed that *The Black Album* would be the last time we would hear JAY-Z on an audio recording. Producers include Kanye West and Just Blaze, but this record will be best remembered for the tracks produced by Dr. Dre, including "Lost One" (co-produced by Mark Batson) and "Minority Report." Each of these songs reveals a more emotionally intelligent, self-reflexive instance of the JAY-Z artistic persona. Because these songs happen to be two of the most compelling performances on the album, they can color the perception of its overall aesthetics and themes. Despite all its critical detractors, *Kingdom Come* must be considered a successful album, selling over 1.5 million copies in a music industry clearly in flux due to technological shifts in distribution methods and platforms.

AMERICAN GANGSTER, Roc-A-Fella/
Def Jam Records, 2007.

Some might say that this is JAY-Z's real comeback album. This concept album, JAY-Z's tenth studio effort, was inspired by the film *American Gangster*, starring Denzel Washington as Harlem drug lord Frank Lucas. The album was released on November 6, 2007. Producers include Diddy and The Hitmen, The Neptunes, No I.D., Jermaine Dupri, and Just Blaze. *American Gangster* probes a coherent and consistent theme of grappling with a hustler's life, his spoils and ills, his hungers and hurts, his desires and disappointments, his traps and triumphs. The musical instrumentation provides a sonic bed to ground the intellectual exploration of a hustler's life and also offers a '70s aesthetic feel to the record. Rapping about gangster themes is nothing new for Jay or his fan base at this time. But the concept of the album, and the compelling corollary experience of viewing the film, helps to distinguish this project within JAY-Z's overall body of work.

THE BLUEPRINT 3. Roc-A-Fella/Def Jam Records, 2009.

The third and likely final installment in JAY-Z's "Blueprint" series of albums was released on September 8, 2009. The album followed the design developed in the first two entries in the series with some remarkable results. "D.O.A. (Death of Auto-Tune)" is a savage attack on the studio enhancement technique that, sadly, continues to dominate rap and popular music. Collaborations with Rihanna and Kanye ("Run This Town"), Drake, J. Cole, Kid Cudi, Pharrell Williams, Jeezy, and others made *The Blueprint 3* Jay's most star-studded project to date. But the artist's favorite song on this record is a collaboration with Alicia Keys—"Empire State of Mind"—a track that must be considered a classic in JAY-Z's considerable oeuvre. It is, remarkably, his first number-one single on the charts as a lead artist. A bevy of established producers contribute to the record, including Timbaland and The Neptunes, but Kanye West and No I.D. account for more than half of its production credits. This album marks JAY-Z's eleventh number-one album according to *Billboard* magazine, thus breaking the record for number-one albums previously held by Elvis Presley.

JAY-Z & Kanye West. *WATCH THE THRONE,* Roc-A-Fella/Roc Nation/Def Jam Records, 2011.

In some ways JAY-Z and Kanye West's collaborative album was over a decade in the making. Since the duo's earliest collaboration on 2000's "This Can't Be Life," and for various tracks on the *Blueprint* (2001) album, West and Pharrell Williams have delivered some of JAY-Z's most memorable production accompaniments. *Watch the Throne* was released on August 8, 2011. The album generally chronicles the duo's extraordinary artistic and financial accomplishments. It celebrates "Black Excellence," and their unique brand of American exceptionalism, even as it questions their presence in such elite spaces. Maturity, accomplishments, wealth, and some social reflection are powerful themes here. West leads a production team of super-producers including Pharrell Williams, Hit-Boy, 88-Keys, Swizz Beatz, and Q-Tip. Successful singles ("Otis") and memorable tracks ("Made in America") abound on *Watch the Throne*. Music videos were created and released for multiple singles. The album received measured critical acclaim and to date has sold over 1.5 million units. The live performances of the album on the "Watch the Throne Tour" became something of a legend, with the breakout, if controversial, single, "Niggas in Paris," being performed over a dozen consecutive times at some shows. The "Watch the Throne Tour" is one of the highest-grossing tours in hip hop history—and a show that I took in three times at three different locations for one of my favorite Jay albums.

MAGNA CARTA HOLY GRAIL, Roc-A-Fella/Roc Nation/ Def Jam Records, 2013.

If you happened to be watching the 2013 NBA Finals, you might have seen a Samsung commercial where JAY-Z announced the release of *Magna Carta Holy Grail* to the world. This release was unique given its initial exclusivity (through a partnership with Samsung, the album was offered to Samsung phone users on July 4, 2013) and its savvy deployment of new streaming technologies that had revolutionized the distribution of popular music. The album was made widely available on July 8, 2013. *Magna Carta* had several successful singles, including "Tom Ford" and "Holy Grail." But in what continues to be one of JAY-Z's most original cinematic contributions to the music video world, the film for "Picasso Baby" emerged as a unique short, paying homage to the classic Marina Abramović installation, "The Artist Is Present." Timbaland is the lead producer on this record with credits on ten of the sixteen tracks. If there was some confusion about which super-producer (West, No I.D., or Timbaland) was going to produce *The Blueprint 3*, it seems that JAY-Z decided to give each a turn at the helm. Other producers on this album include Mike Will Made It, Pharrell Williams, and Jerome "J-Roc" Harmon.

4:44, Roc Nation, 2017.

4:44 was released on June 30, 2017, through an exclusive partnership between Sprint and JAY-Z's streaming service, TIDAL. This is far and away JAY-Z's most personal, and private, record to date. It could be argued that it is more of a Shawn Carter record than a JAY-Z product. The title refers either to a predawn moment in which Carter was inspired to write the title track, one of the most sincere and personal records he has ever written, or it is a sly reference to the address of the Standard Hotel (444 West 13th Street) where the infamous elevator confrontation between him and sister-in-law Solange occurred. Or it's an allusion to both. *4:44* is about life, family, regret, and redemption. Here JAY-Z is not afraid to show how he feels about his love life or the politics of race in America. "The Story of O.J.," and its attendant animated music video, is one of Jay's most direct forays into the world of American racial politics. It is a stunning achievement both lyrically and visually. Several music videos accompany this record, including visuals for "MaNyfaCed-God" and "Kill Jay Z." (Note the artist's new spelling, "JAY-Z," symbolically killing "Jay Z.") The music video for "Family Feud," with a Flying Lotus score, was directed by the enormously gifted Ava DuVernay. No I.D. produces the entire album along with JAY-Z himself, and James Blake, Dominic Maker, and Mount Kimbie earned a few co-producer credits along the way.

ACKNOWLEDGMENTS

Yo, I'm gon' spit these acknowledgments

Like hip hop was always meant

To heal the breach between emotion and emolument

(When I first learned that word from Du Bois it seemed heaven sent)

First off, I got to thank my editor Elisabeth Dyssegaard

The perfect guard of my literary art

To finish from start with such vision and heart

And to the greatest literary agent in the land

Tanya McKinnon got the canon in hand

Never shootin' blanks when she got her cerebral cannon in hand

Like my man, Alan Bradshaw, he's no Stan

When it comes to taking a grammatical stand

Make them sentences land perfectly in this verbal gymnastic stand

And countless thanks to the ladies who feed this nice rhyme

Jen Enderlin, my publisher, is my partner in crime

No really, she is, we spit Godfather lines

While she signs off on my most challenging lines

Laura Clark, her captain at sea, sails right on through

Takes books to market and makes them do what they do

And the Grand Dame Sally Richardson always comes through

Her blood royal blue, her vision so true

And because of the real Godfather, Don Weisberg, I can ball

His faith in me at St. Martin's really started it all

He gets in the foxhole and doesn't lurk in the hall

Gabi Gantz, my lively publicist, keeps my name in the press

And Martin Quinn, my marvelous marketer, makes it all look fresh

And to Lena Shekhter, with your production I can say we are blessed

Jennifer Fernandez edits that production the best

To David Rotstein that cover you designed is a straight up classic

To Jennifer Simington, you may have copyedited us into a classic

And Steven Seighman, that dope text design will leave all readers ecstatic

To Killer Mike, Marc Lamont Hill and James Braxton Peterson

Y'all put me on to Jay when I had only paid attention to God's son

That changed my mind, made me realize the full sweep of Hov's genius

Thank you Hov for letting me sample these words, oh yes you're a genius

(You and Queen Bey, despite us trying to tell you, have no idea what you mean to us)

To Pharrell for that magical Foreword and for offering your trust

That these pages I wrote are rhetorically just

Thanks to Desiree Perez, mighty Boss Lady, and Jana Fleishman, sublime ruler of pub

Appreciate that COO support and introducing me to your amazing club

Marie Plaisime and Peterson put in the research to help me craft this book

Plaisime did work in class and searched through them books

Peterson supplied me with words, wit and wisdom and countless rhetorical hooks

Michelle Jean-Paul kept me up on social media and showed the big brain it took

To write those words with all the scholarship and love that it took

Thanks to legends Quest Love, Queen Latifah, Skip Gates and Rev. Al Sharpton too

Gifted lady Tamron Hall and my man Common too

(One of the illest rappers to ever bless us with the knowledge that you do)

To Spike Lee and Tyler Perry, great men, for the seeds that you sowed

Thanks to all of you for them blurbs and the love that y'all showed

And to my precious loving family that helps carry the load

My nieces and nephew, my cousins, aunts and uncles all

My grandkids, grandnephews and grandnieces—all y'all

(Whaddup grandies Layla, Mosi and Max, growing so tall)

My great sons Mike and Mwata, my daughter Maisha, hey boo

My Mama Addie Mae for the love you give to all

(And Mama Susan Taylor, Big Brother Khephra Burns, my dear friends

Lost my brother Everett Dyson-Bey, spent 30 years in the pen

But nothing can kill your memory that means so much to us in the end

I got your only son Everett Dyson brilliantly illustrating with his pen

That boy so good I got to work with him again

My brothers Brian and Gregory still got mad love for these men

And to the Grandest Matriarch of them all we give you your just due

Activist and speaker, brilliant writer, the glue

Marcia Louise Dyson, we love you for all that you do

BIBLIOGRAPHY

Chapter 1

Walter McDougall, *Freedom Just Around the Corner: A New American History, 1585–1828* (New York: Harper, 2004).

Tatiana Adeline Thieme, "The Hustle Economy: Informality, Uncertainty and the Geographies of Getting By," *Progress in Human Geography* (February 2017).

Mike Davis, *City of Quartz: Excavating the Future in Los Angeles* (New York: Verso, 1990).

Khalil Gibran Muhammad, "Playing the Violence Card," *New York Times*, April 5, 2012.

Jay-Z, *Decoded* (New York: Spiegel & Grau, 2010).

Chapter 2

Jay-Z, *Decoded* (New York: Spiegel & Grau, 2010).

Imani Perry, "Putting the 'Public' in 'Public Intellectual,'" *Chronicle of Higher Education*, June 6, 2010.

"Oprah Talks to Jay-Z," *O* magazine, October 2009, https://www

.oprah.com/omagazine/oprah-interviews-jay-z-october-2009-issue-of
-o-magazine/.

Albert "Prodigy" Johnson, *My Infamous Life: The Autobiography of Mobb Deep's Prodigy* (New York: Touchstone, 2011).

Chapter 3

Shawn Carter, "Jay Z: For Father's Day, I'm Taking On the Exploitative Bail Industry," *Time,* June 16, 2017, https://time.com/4821547 /jay-z-racism-bail-bonds/.

Jay-Z, "Jay-Z: The Criminal Justice System Stalks Black People Like Meek Mill," *New York Times,* November 17, 2017.

REFORM Alliance, "REFORM Alliance & Pennsylvania State Representatives Unveil Bipartisan Legislation to Reform State Probation & Parole System," press release, *PRNewsWire,* https://www.prnewswire.com /news-releases/reform-alliance—pennsylvania-state-representatives -unveil-bipartisan-legislation-to-reform-state-probation—parole -system-300823231.html.

Bill Cosby, "Address at the NAACP' on the 50th Anniversary of *Brown v. Board of Education*," speech, May 17, 2004, Constitution Hall, Washington, D.C.

Michael Eric Dyson, *Mercy, Mercy Me: The Art, Loves and Demons of Marvin Gaye* (New York: Basic Books, 2004).

Michael Eric Dyson, *Is Bill Cosby Right?: Or Has the Black Middle Class Lost Its Mind?* (New York: Basic Civitas Books, 2005).

David Garrow, "The Troubling Legacy of Martin Luther King," *Standpoint,* May 30, 2019, https://standpointmag.co.uk/issues/june -2019/the-troubling-legacy-of-martin-luther-king/.

David Garrow, *Bearing the Cross: Martin Luther King, Jr., and the Southern Christian Leadership Conference* (New York: HarperCollins, 1986).

Taylor Branch, *At Canaan's Edge: America in the King Years, 1965–68* (New York: Simon & Schuster, 2006).

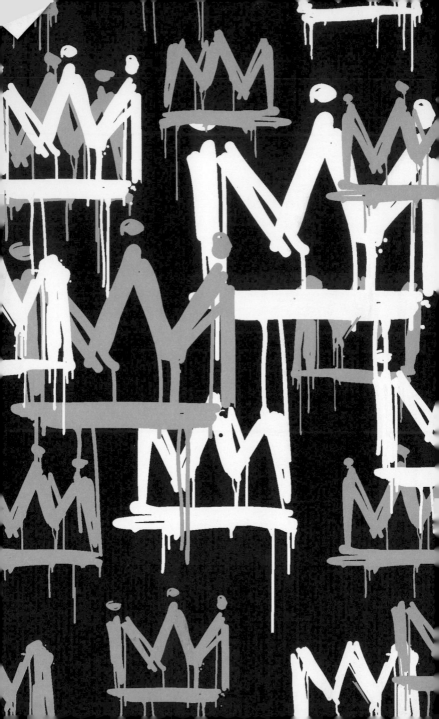